Melvyn Matthews is Chancellor Emeritus of Wells Cathedral, where he had responsibility for the cathedral's programme of education and spirituality. He also oversaw the Ministry of Welcome to the many visitors the cathedral receives. For some time, he was the Senior Chaplain to Bristol University but, before that, taught in the Department of Theology and Religious Studies in the University of Nairobi. More recently, Canon Matthews was the Director of the Ammerdown Centre, an ecumenical laity centre near Bath. He has written a number of books, the most recent being *Lit by the Light of God: Prayers and Meditations through the Year*, *Both Alike to Thee: The Retrieval of the Mystical Way* and *Nearer than Breathing: Biblical Reflections on God's Involvement in Us* (published by SPCK). He is co-author of *Wells Cathedral* (published by Scala). He is married with children and grandchildren, and enjoys sailing.

D1434728

AWAKE TO GOD

Explorations in the Mystical Way

Melvyn Matthews

First published in Great Britain in 2006

Society for Promoting Christian Knowledge
36 Causton Street
London SW1P 4ST

The author and publisher gratefully acknowledge permission to
reproduce copyright material:
On page 94, Edwin Muir, 'The Transfiguration', from *Collected Poems 1921–58*,
Faber & Faber, 1960.
On pages 103 and 104, Paul Celan, 'Tenebrae' and 'Psalm', from *Selected Poems and
Prose of Paul Celan*, translated by John Felstiner. Copyright © 2001 by John Felstiner.
Used by permission of W. W. Norton & Company, Inc.
On page 113, Philip Lyons, an unpublished poem about Etty Hillesum.

Every effort has been made to acknowledge fully the sources of material reproduced in
this book. The publisher apologizes for any omissions that may remain and, if notified,
will ensure that full acknowledgements are made in a subsequent edition.

Scripture quotations are from the New Revised Standard Version of the Bible,
Anglicized Edition, copyright © 1989, 1995 by the Division of Christian Education
of the National Council of the Churches of Christ in the USA. Used by permission.

British Library Cataloguing-in-Publication Data
A catalogue record for this book is available from the British Library

ISBN-13: 978–0–281–05801–3
ISBN-10: 0–281–05801–6

1 3 5 7 9 10 8 6 4 2

Typeset by Graphicraft Limited, Hong Kong
Printed in Great Britain by Ashford Colour Press

We infinitely wrong ourselves by laziness and confinement. All creatures in all nations, and tongues, and people praise God infinitely; and the more, for being your sole and perfect treasures. You are never what you ought till you go out of yourself and walk among them.

Thomas Traherne, *Centuries of Meditations*, 2.76

Contents

Preface

This book is the result of time spent reflecting on our contemporary spiritual condition and its relationship to the Christian mystical tradition. Its genesis is, perhaps, in an occasion I can still remember, when as a university chaplain I tried to talk to students about St John of the Cross and the negative way and was faced with total incomprehension and accusations of trying to drag the Church back into the Middle Ages! My reaction was to go back to the texts and to try to see what they really meant. Meanwhile much has happened in the academic world in the understanding of mystical texts, particularly over the last ten or fifteen years, and these developments are unfortunately little known in the mainstream of the Christian Church. As I read I realized that these developments were just what I needed! So over the years I have set myself the personal task of making the mystical texts part of the understanding of the contemporary Church and I have been infinitely helped in that process by the academic work of people like Mark McIntosh, Bernard McGinn and Denys Turner among others. My task, as John Arnold, later Dean of Durham, once told me, has been that of *haute vulgarisation*, making available and accessible the work of others. I have always aimed to speak to our present with good news from the past and to make the past tradition available and relevant to today's seeker. So this book is both a pastoral and an academic exercise: pastoral because it tries to suggest a style of being and seeing for the contemporary Christian, an answer to the question 'How can we be a Christian today?'; and academic because it finds much support in that task from recent research into mystical texts which brings them really alive for people now. So the book aims to stimulate reflection on our present spiritual condition and at the same time to stimulate study of a small number of particular writers who interest me and who I judge to be of special help in that process of reflection because the situations they faced in the past and the way forward they provided then are relevant to us today. In each case knowledge of recent research into these writers enables us to view them in a new light and sharpens their relevance to us.

Usually these writers are seen as 'spiritual', and they are often quoted, or their example trotted out by those who are involved in the contemporary explosion in spirituality. The difficulty is that those who do this are often ignorant of what these writers were trying to do in their own time and so use them out of context, and their truth is distorted and lost. For example, Eckhart is often seen as 'a mystic', whatever that means; but recent research shows that Eckhart had a very critical understanding of so-called 'mystical' developments in his own day, especially among the Beguines with whom he worked, which meant that his theology became a critique of certain types of what we would call 'mysticism'. This critique is very relevant to today's situation, which needs to look more carefully than it does at the term 'spirituality'. Similarly, contemporary work on Julian of Norwich shows that her real relevance to contemporary Christians is to do with the Christian relationship to the 'body' of church and state in which we live rather than simply providing a boost to Christian feminism (which it also does). The recent discovery of new manuscripts by Thomas Traherne brings him into a new focus. Contemporary commentary is now able to deconstruct Traherne out of the 'spirituality' scene much more effectively than we were able with only the text of the *Centuries of Meditations* to hand. Etty Hillesum is often quoted by those on the feminist scene, but scant attention is paid to her relationship to post-Holocaust theology, which is why I have grouped her with Paul Celan, the principal poet of the Holocaust. They are both writers who, from within the Jewish tradition, and as a result of their time spent facing horror, raise the question of how we may speak about God in a time when traditional ways of speech are no longer available to us.

This brings us to an underlying theme of the book which is the question of how we can do theology in a postmodern situation. The book wishes to say something about 'postmodernism' and what it means. In one sense all of us are postmodernists now. This is often seen by traditionalists as a threat to the meta-narrative which classical Christianity espouses, but this book wishes to demonstrate that postmodernism is not the threat to faith that some Christians believe it to be. It believes that the postmodern condition enables us to reaffirm central Christian truths, but in a totally new way which 'postmodern' people can, perhaps, accept. It does this in particular by focusing on the issue of the self and showing that the self is essentially participatory rather than ontological. If we are to be who we were made to be then we are to 'wake up' to different possibilities. This awakening or 'self-forgetting' enables us to believe in God and to take on board traditional doctrines, but it has to occur first. The spiritual writers who are dealt with in the book all accepted this in one degree or another, mostly (perhaps with the exception of Julian) without making any issue of it whatsoever. This brings them into a clear relationship with postmodernist theologians. So, hanging about behind this book are the insights of a number of postmodern theologians such as Jean Luc Marion and Emmanuel Levinas.

So I have attempted, perhaps rashly, but I hope creatively, to bring together the different themes of self-emptying and participation which postmodern theologians have brought back into the conversation about God, and relate those insights to the Christian mystical tradition and combine them with the insights of that tradition to suggest a style of being and seeing for the contemporary Christian. Unfortunately I find that this is seriously different from many of the contemporary British, especially the contemporary evangelical, attempts to state the faith. I believe, however, that it actually meets current criticisms of Christianity as being too dogmatic or doctrinal in a radically different way. This book presents the faith as something which indeed may even not look properly theistic or christocentric enough to some, but it is I believe actually a way of practising the faith that replicates Christ in the world by means of the sacrificial participatory and enraptured self which is ready to go out of itself in order to become itself. Merely thinking about Christian doctrine does not do that. This should provide a way forward into the faith for those who do not feel able to espouse the statements of the faith currently on offer, however dressed up they might be.

The book began as a set of lectures given in Wells Cathedral during Lent 2004 when I was the Canon Chancellor and the Acting Dean there. I am grateful to Prebendary Graham Dodds and Canon Russell Bowman Eadie for help and advice particularly over the use of PowerPoint technology and to the Virgers of Wells Cathedral, especially Tim Jones, for valuable assistance during the presentations. Naturally the original lectures have developed considerably since they were first given, and I would like to thank Benedicte Scholefield, the Director of the Ammerdown Centre, and Dr Tim McQuiban, the Principal of Sarum College, for the opportunity to try them out upon people in their establishments. These occasions gave me the opportunity to reflect and to develop my thinking. My wife June has, of course, been totally encouraging and supportive, especially as I faced writing them up in the early days of my retirement. The book is dedicated to her with thankfulness.

Melvyn Matthews

1

The promise of postmodernity

'God calls. He calls always. His call is personal and universal.'
With these words the priest began the mass. They were words
which seemed to come from somewhere else, from outside of
the church, from deep within the being of the worshippers, from
another place. The words were repeated, it seemed, by the light
entering the building and speaking to us as it fell through
the triforium windows. 'God calls . . .' The music also, simple
haunting chants, and the studied simplicity of the movements
of the liturgy, spoke of a call from elsewhere coming into the
ground of our beings which were open to hear. The space and
light, the clarity and simplicity of the music, the silences, all
embodied the space in the human person which was waiting
to hear this word out of silence, the call of God, and waited
to respond in an answering cry, 'I hear you even though I see
you not . . .'

We were at mass in the great basilica at Vézelay in France.
The mass was being celebrated on an early autumn Sunday
morning by the Communities of Jerusalem, men and women
given to hearing the voice of God in the heart of the desert which
is symbolized by the modern city. The clarity and simplicity of
the liturgical movements, the words spoken, the things unsaid,
possessed an enormous impact. It seemed as if an ancient
voice was being spoken again in this place. With the opening
words of the priest the Christian tradition, with all of its complexities and the weight of its inheritance, simplified itself. So
much was laid aside. Only what was necessary emerged and spoke

to the many hundreds gathered there, many hundreds who were wrapped and entangled in the fragmentations of the modern world, who were enmeshed in the myriad choices that such a broken world presents.

What was not presented was a repetition of old truths. Neither the introductory words of the priest nor his sermon affirmed certain intellectual or propositional truths. All was derived from the dynamism of God's call and a response to that summons. We were asked to enter into the silence of trust. Nor could hierarchy be perceived. There was no place or insignia for a prior or abbot. The community members were dressed alike. Men and women together distributed the Eucharist. There were no processions of hierarchical order. There was no choir which knew or sang music which the people did not know or sing. There was no anthem to listen to. Everything was open to everybody present. Nor did the Christian past lay a heavy hand over the occasion. The Nicene Creed was sung lyrically by all as an affirmation rather than a set of intellectual or pro-positional truths. There was nothing over against you. There was nothing to obstruct the word emerging out of silence. The call could be heard.

This mass was a response to the postmodern condition which inhabits all of us now. In itself it was also postmodern. That was why it could speak so clearly to those who came. It did not try to recreate Christendom or assert eternal and fundamental verities of a particular kind. It lived with and expressed itself within the terms of the postmodern condition. The word 'postmodern' is no more than shorthand for the pre-sent fragmented condition of humanity in the western world. This fragmented condition has come about because the mod-ern world – once hailed as that which would release us all from the slavery of the past – produces as many difficulties as it does benefits. The rise of the modern since the Renaissance and the Enlightenment appeared inexorable and good. It has brought immense benefits – medical, scientific and technological – and these are evident for all to see and for so many to enjoy. Without the progress of the modern world we would all still be caught in the poverty of the medieval period. What, however, has become clear in the latter half of the twentieth century is that while the modern world has brought benefits, these do not automatically extend to all. Indeed they are present for some only because others have been deprived of the resources which have been necessary to develop them. Moreover, some see the violence, both physical and economic, which modern nations have visited upon themselves and upon others as being a direct consequence of the development of modern technology. Others see such violence as deriving from the inability of powerful western nations to abandon their imperialist mindset. The consequence of this is that we are now no longer part of a single culture. We are not easily part of a single tradition. We have lost confidence in the securities of the past and in the framework which the past gave us. There is now no single story which inhabits us, or at least there is now no single story which inhabits us automatically. We have to create or reach out for an overarching story or 'metanarrative' as it is called. We cannot rely on it being there without us. We are left, as stuttering and groping blind people, reaching out either to recreate the past or to build modern castles in the air.

Many believe that to do either is impossible. The past cannot be recreated without imposing alien values upon ourselves or upon others. The future cannot be envisaged because there are no sure principles upon which to build. We simply have to accept the inconsequential nature of the present. There is nothing. In reaction to such apparent cynicism many in the Church assert fundamental truths. Nor is the Christian Church the only body to be afflicted with the need to make such a move. It affects all faiths and all political and ideological bodies. Politics as well as religion is riven with the divisions between the traditionalists and the modernizers, both of whom are in reaction to the present fragmentation. The real

3

question is not which of them is right, for indeed neither of them is right. The battle cannot be resolved in the terms in which it is set. The real question is whether we can see that our present condition, which we believe to be an affliction, is actually a gift, a moment in which we can rediscover our capacity to see and respond to the immensity of God. In the apparent emptiness of the present God calls and asks us to listen. A word emerges out of the silence.

That should really be enough, but there is more to it than that. Understanding that the postmodern condition represents an opportunity to recover faith in life as gift, and so the gift of love from God, means that postmodernity is not the threat that many perceive it to be. Postmodernity should enable us to reaffirm central Christian truths but in a different way, but in order to see how this might happen we have to say a little more about the postmodern condition. How did it arise and what does it mean? Postmodernity has been described as a type of cyberspace, the virtual reality inhabited by the internet. Here there are apparently no boundaries. Things happen within no time and communication is continuous. Here there is no single principled standpoint from which to observe things, observation as such is meaningless, participation is all. Identity is not substantial. Who or what you are is determined by the position or viewpoint you have been occupying until that moment and that can and does change constantly. Identity is relative to the circumstance or position of the moment. There is no commitment to one thing; what is good is what is useful. It has also been noted that such a condition can, like the virtual reality of cyberspace, only be entered by those with sufficient financial capacity. Postmodernity is a function of so-called advanced western societies where wealth enables choice and where the marketing of products becomes the central reality rather than the product which is being marketed. The cult film *The Matrix* illustrates the difference between the modern and the postmodern. The film portrays an individual caught in the virtual reality of an enormous computer network. Here there is no individuality, for all individuals are part of the network. This network is being subverted from outside by a group of people who live in real time and who have a real capacity for choice. The battle is between these two different 'layers' of existence, the modern, with its slightly cranky and cantankerous people operating real machines, and the postmodern, where all is part of the whole and all in thrall to the network as a whole.

In this film the two realities are parallel. In history they are consequential. The modern arises with the European Renaissance. Here in the fifteenth and sixteenth centuries perspective in art and architecture is rediscovered after being lost with the demise of the classical world. Physical space, time and matter are described and measured by empirical means. Bodies begin to be looked at, medical textbooks are written and the measurement of time means that clocks and watches become important and the calendar can be changed, as it was in 1582. Galileo said at this time,

> I think that in discussing natural problems we should not begin from the authority of scriptural passages, but from sensory experiences and necessary demonstrations.

So in a real sense the 'modern' is truly modern. It is not something which has come to us always. As the modern period progresses and the Renaissance moves inexorably into the Reformation and the Enlightenment, two further characteristics of the truly modern move to the fore. These are belief in the centrality of reason and belief in progress, which many people also believed to be inevitable.

During the twentieth century this overall self-understanding, one which has brought untold benefits to so many, began to break down. There is terrible conflict between nations. There is increasing division between rich and poor, both individually and nationally. Progress, thought by so many to be inevitable, has not always come to all, and even when it has, further unseen problems and horrors have arisen to accompany it. Moreover, the very benefits which modernism has produced for so many have also been used to allow or facilitate genocide. This is why the Holocaust was a particularly 'modern' phenomenon. Here there was pride in the fact that the trains taking so many to their deaths ran on time and here modern manufacturing processes were used to annihilate millions of people. By the end of the twentieth century so many felt that the development of modernism had resulted in a disenchanted, efficient world run for the benefit of the successful and rich.

It is, therefore, not surprising that after the Second World War and in the wake of the apparent emptiness of modernity, there should arise in Europe an attempt to understand things differently, a way of seeing which articulated the condition in which humanity, or at least postmodern European humanity, found itself. This 'way of seeing' is expressed differently by different thinkers, but one of its primary characteristics is a serious questioning of one of modernisms central affirmations, the centrality of the self. Is there really a self, an 'I' around which existence can be ordered? It seems to many postmodern thinkers that the insistence upon the centrality of the ego-self has resulted in so many difficulties that its existence is best questioned or ignored. Alongside this questioning of the centrality of the self there has arisen a questioning of the central place of reason in human affairs. For the postmodern thinker reason is associated with power and control and it is clearly the exercise of power and control which has done so much harm in contemporary human affairs. But the demotion of the ego-self and reason is not simply a negative move, for such a demotion then allows the return of the imagination and metaphor as primary means of communication. Truth can now occur in different forms. The truth of metaphor and symbol becomes at least as important as the truth revealed by logic or reason. Emmanuel Levinas, for example, one of the leading postmodern philosophers, speaks of how images work on the human consciousness, saying that they possess a mode of being in which 'the I is stripped of its prerogative to assume'. He says, 'An image does not engender a conception, as do scientific cognition and truth . . . An image marks a hold over us rather than our initiative'. For Levinas, 'art turns the sovereign ego out of its house'[1] and enables human beings to concentrate on what he calls the ethical.

A further aspect of the postmodern way of seeing is that if there is now a serious question-mark over understanding the world solely according to reason and what the individual human ego can know, then the unknown nature of the other person, his or her difference or separateness, becomes important. Levinas calls this otherness 'alterity'. This can be illustrated from Shakespeare's treatment of Othello, the Moor of Venice. Most people would say that Othello murders Desdemona because he believed that he knew she had been unfaithful. He is prompted to this by his own capacity for jealousy which is fired by the intrigues of sly Iago; but above all he believed he knew what she had done. The moral of this type of tragedy consists in the fact that we cannot ultimately know everything about the other person, even, and perhaps especially, if the other person is someone that we love. This means that in our relationships with other people we have to learn to acknowledge what we cannot know. Failure to acknowledge this was Othello's tragic flaw. Of course that flaw was fuelled by a number of further factors – his maleness – alpha males must *know* – and by his race, for he had to prove to white people, especially the aristocracy of Venice who employed him, that he knew. But basically he thought he knew. He was trapped in his need for certainty. The end of certainty is the beginning of trust, and so the beginning of wholesome ethical relationships, but Othello was unable to trust.

Postmodernity insists that we have to respect the separateness or the transcendence of the other person. Each of us has to acknowledge that there are bounds or limits to our knowledge of the other. There is a secretness about the other which human beings find difficult to acknowledge. At the primary level this secrecy is to do with ethics and how we behave. The source of a truly ethical relationship with another does not so much lie in our ability to know and choose what we have to do, but more in our capacity to face the other and allow the other in all their difference to face me. At that point I – and hopefully the other person – will acknowledge that the other holds within them a difference and that this difference is not totally known. This will enable respect and prevent dangerous and, in Othello's case, murderous assumptions being made. Human prejudice does not do this. Anti-Semitism is a willing disregard of what we do not know about Jews. The Nazis believed that they *knew* that Jews were not really human and *knew* that they could prove this scientifically. Prejudice against women is a refusal to take the otherness and transcendence of women seriously.

Perhaps this short and inadequate look at one or two of the major elements in a postmodernist way of seeing things will enable the reader to see not just how and why it has developed but also some of the consequences which it brings. In literature, for example, the postmodern abandonment of the centrality of the all-seeing human ego enables the postmodern novelist to play with different perspectives in the development of a story. A recent example of this can be found in the different endings of Ian MacEwan's acclaimed novel *Atonement*. The disconcerting question is raised as to whether the account we have followed was the true or only account of the events stemming from that fateful day in 1935 or whether our understanding was limited and partial. Abandonment of the centrality of the 'I' enables the postmodern literary critic to ask whether any work of literature has what has conventionally been understood to be 'an author'. Is not any work of literature the product of the conditions prevalent at the time whoever the 'author' is? How important is the concept of the 'author' anyway? Can such a concept not obstruct or limit our understanding of a particular work and, by concentrating on the author's self-perceived intentions, prevent us from seeing the invisible social influences at work in the production of this book? In science the postmodern scientist is now able to take on board different types of explanations, explanations which work at different levels for different phenomena. No longer is there a single scientific view about how things are. Quantum theory works as well as Newtonian physics and the Indeterminacy Principle arises as the supreme postmodern scientific explanation.

But what about religion? Is postmodernism any assistance to the life of faith? What are the consequences of the rise of postmodernism for the person of faith? Or is postmodernism destructive of faith because faith implies a constant and single explanation of things, the 'truth' of the Bible or the Church or Christian doctrine, while postmodernism questions or denies all of these things? To see how postmodernism is of real assistance to the life of faith we must return first of all to the question of the unknown nature of the other. Postmodernism would say that this acknowledgement of the otherness or difference of the other person is not just an insight into human relationships; it is an insight into how things are as a whole. A religious person can build on this and say that it is not just an insight into how reality is constructed, but above all it is an insight into the nature of faith and so a gateway to faith in the unknown one who is God. By opening ourselves to the unknown we open ourselves to God. So it is an insight fundamental to a true faith.

Let us look for a moment at one or two of the founding moments of faith in the Hebrew scriptures. These are to be found in the book Exodus in chapter 20 and the chapters thereabout. Here, under the guise of a historical narrative about the giving of the law, which to a certain extent it is, we have a mythical or archetypal account of our human condition. These are the founding myths which tell us who we are before God. They work at the deepest level of truth which lies beyond the merely historical. What happens at the beginning of Hebrew religion is that Moses has to come to terms with the unknown nature of God. There are several passages which reflect this, including the one about God's name – 'Who shall I tell them sent me?' – where Moses has to go back to the people with no 'name', just 'I AM WHO I AM'.[2] The incident I want to focus on concerns the darkness of God. At one point during the giving of the law in Exodus Moses asks to see the glory of God, 'Show me your glory, I pray.' But this is refused. God says, 'I will make all my goodness pass before you ... But ... you cannot see my face; for no one shall see me and live.' And then there is that wonderful passage where God places Moses in a cleft of the rock, 'and I will cover you with my hand until I have passed by; then I will take away my hand, and you shall see my back; but my face shall not be seen'.[3] And everything else stems from this. Moses and the children of Israel have to go on into the wilderness without knowing where they are going. There are explicit moments when the darkness of trust becomes too difficult and they rebel, asking to be taken back to the certainties of Egypt. When they are settled in the Promised Land the same difficulty assails them. They cannot deal with a God they cannot see and regularly turn to the gods of other nations whom they believe they can see. An unknown God who does not have a specific name ('I am who I am') and who hides himself is not easy to deal with. They have real trouble with the darkness of trust and it is to this that the prophets constantly recall them. There is little consolation in prophetic religion, little to reassure or provide comfort, nothing much to prove to you that God is. You have to remain in an attitude of trust, believing that the God of Abraham, Isaac and Jacob is God. The consolations of religion are provided by the gods of other nations. Israel's God was not visible.

But not only was he invisible, he was also terrifying. In the beginning God spoke. Indeed, he spoke to us and with us. That much is clear from Genesis where God comes to converse with his children in the garden at the time of the evening breeze. But even there, right at the beginning, something has happened which made conversation difficult. There is a fear and a hiding involved for Adam says, 'I heard the sound of you in the garden, and I was afraid . . .'[4] So even at the beginning humankind finds it difficult to face God and speak with him. But it gets worse, for in Exodus chapter 20 there is a complete breakdown in the conversation. At the giving of the law on Mount Sinai there are a lot of words and a lot of noise and the text says, 'When all the people witnessed the thunder and lightning, the sound of the trumpet, and the mountain smoking, they were afraid and trembled and stood at a distance, and said to Moses, "You speak to us, and we will listen; but do not let God speak to us, or we will die." '[5] And, of course, this is not the only moment of terror before God in the Old Testament, nor, for that matter, the New. The prophets were only too conscious of the terrifying nature of God. We do not have to go further than the visions of Isaiah or Ezekiel or Daniel to see this. And it is no use saying that this is Old Testament religion about fear which has been replaced by the comforting Good News of Jesus, for we know very well how he speaks hard words to those who have come without wedding garments – but above all how he calls his disciples to follow him into the darkness and terror of Jerusalem where they do not easily follow. This inability to cope with the terrifying darkness of God is recorded most explicitly in the New Testament in Mark's Gospel – the one John Fenton calls 'the oldest and the best'[6] – and Mark's Gospel ends with the words 'and they said nothing to anyone, for they were afraid'.[7] But it is not just the resurrection which is terrifying in Mark's account but also the crucifixion. John Fenton points out that there are distinct parallels between Jesus' self-offering and the terrifying story of the sacrifice of Isaac by Abraham. Fenton says, 'When we get to the second half of Mark's book we are told straight off, "The son

11

of man must suffer and everyone who wants to be a follower must also suffer". "Everyone will be salted with fire".[8] The problem for Mark was that not only the disciples in the story but also his readers could not accept that. It was too terrifying – hence the addition of consoling endings to Mark later than the ending at chapter 16 verse 8, hence the writing of other Gospels – Matthew and especially Luke – where the sense of terror about the encounter with the original Jesus is softened or lost. But even then this sense of terror about God does not go away but crops up again later in the New Testament in the Letter to the Hebrews where it is clear that our God is a consuming fire.

These texts from the Hebrew and Christian scriptures are actually, first of all, texts about human consciousness. Human consciousness is enormous and profound. It is aware of death and tragedy and enormous joy and the enormous and over-whelming weal and woe of being alive now. It is aware of the invisibility and terror of being alive. Sebastian Faulks's over-whelming novel *Human Traces* is an attempt to look at the his-tory of what it means to be mad. In the process of tracing that history through the friendship of two pioneering psychiatrists Faulks conveys something of the enormity of being alive, something of the horror and the holiness of it all. At several points in the novel the principal character, Thomas, is like Moses for he stands before the terrible invisibility of things and speaks of their holiness. This happens at several points in the novel but most markedly when he gives a paper which sum-marizes his life's quest for cures to human madness – a quest which has seen very little in the way of results. He talks in a remarkably postmodern manner about how the insoluble knots and mysteries of life will be resolved not by finding an 'answer' but by developing 'a different perspective', and he concludes.

> I ask you to believe that we are the most fortunate species ever
> to have lived or that it is possible to conceive of existing – ever,

in this universe or in any other; and that it is our duty each
day therefore to appreciate our astonishing good fortune by
caring for the insane who pay the price for all of us, and
by turning our healthy lives, so near as we can manage it, day
by day, into an extended rapture.[9]

This is a truly postmodern perspective. One might even
suspect Sebastian Faulks, when he makes Thomas speak of
'rapture', of having read the accounts of what some postmodern philosophers call 'jouissance', that is joy and delight in
all things. But it is also a basic faith perspective. Although Thomas
avows that he is an unbeliever he does allow the possibility
that those who believe in a 'higher outside force' can come to
the same conclusion. His paper is not accepted by his hearers,
even by his closest colleague, because they are like Othello,
they cannot cope with the terror of the unknown. They insist
on answers. What people of faith would claim is that when
Thomas speaks of his rapture before the unknown he is talking about the same thing as they are when they speak of their
faith. What people like Thomas know about life and what the
tradition of faith says about life are the same things and effectively it is only the rise of the postmodern mentality which has
allowed us to see this. The terror and invisibility of life that many
have experienced and what Christians have been talking about
for two thousand years is the same thing. It is not perceived
as the same thing because most people's eyes are prejudiced
against the perceptions of faith and because people of faith,
the supposed guardians of the unknown, the invisible and the
terrifying, have been talking for too long about proofs and
answers, often because they think that modernism, with its
attempts to find answers, is the only real truth. The arrival of
the postmodern should release believers from such stupidity.

So the first thing that living in a postmodern environment
should do is to provide believers with the conditions under which
a more authentic faith is possible. This is a faith which faces

13

the unknowns of existence, including the apparent absence of God, and instead of seeking for answers, as the modern age did, gives thanks for what is and allows an extended rapture to triumph. But as soon as that is said then others will rejoin that this is not the traditional Christian faith as we have known it, it is no more than the possibility of faith. What about the basic Christian doctrines, the incarnation, the Trinity, the sacraments, do they survive in this environment or are they now redundant, either because they are illogical or because they are inadequate verbal responses to a more overwhelming rapture? Is it enough simply to talk about the possibility of faith in a postmodern age? Perhaps not. So more must be done. It is at this point that the postmodern understanding of the self becomes important. We have said that the postmodern thinker, because of the damage that he has seen imposed upon others by those who believe in the human ego-self, has abandoned such a view. This is largely true, but we have not said clearly what has replaced this view. What has emerged is a view of the self as essentially participatory. We are what we are because we live and move within a complex of other personalities who have made and continue to make us what we are. Emmanuel Levinas, for example, refuses the traditional definitions of the self. We are not an instance of some general concept or genus of the human being, an ego or self-consciousness or thinking being. For him the abstract choosing willing ego is replaced by 'me', by the one who responds to the call and question of the other. The human being's first word is not 'cogito ergo sum', I think therefore I am, but, in French 'me voici', 'here I am', or 'see me here'. This is in fact the term which the prophets use in responding to the call of God in the Hebrew Scriptures, 'Here I am'. In other words identity is only constituted in response to the call of the mysterious other, both the other person and the God who hides within the call of the other. We are only real when we say 'Here I am'. If that is the case then what human beings are is a set of relationships. Once that is established then the faithful person can be released into belief in the traditional Christian doctrines with a new energy and a new joy. The reason for that is that the traditional doctrines are themselves to do with participation. While they appear to be paradoxical or even irrational they are only so when viewed from a purely rational perspective and questions are asked such as 'How can three be one?' or 'How can two natures exist within one person?' These are questions to which there is no answer unless we change our perspective. What does enable us to change our perspective is first of all a realization that such questions assume that the human identity of Jesus is that of a separate conscious self, that he has an ego-self which cannot easily be shared. Once we realize that human identity is not like that then the problem begins to unravel itself. If we could see human identity in terms of relationships then that might give us a better window into the doctrines we profess to hold. But another part of the jigsaw about believing in the Trinity, for example, falls into place when we understand how recent research understands the terms which are used. Most contemporary theologians of the Trinity are now agreed that in the classical formulations of the doctrine by Augustine or by Thomas Aquinas, there is no warrant for saying that there are three 'persons' in God, especially when you mean by 'person' three individual subjects or centres of consciousness. The three *personae* are simply the three ways in which God's single self-consciousness is aware and the three ways in which humans respond to his call. So we are not isolated subjects but persons who are only persons when we are visited or, in Levinas's terms, 'called', by the other. When we understand ourselves in this way we will not only have a happier view of ourselves but will also be able to return to faith in a Trinitarian God and know that we can respond to and participate in his life. The same process occurs when we attempt to re-understand the doctrines of the incarnation and the atonement. The postmodern climate allows these doctrines to live again and releases us from puzzling over their meaning and vainly trying to impart that meaning to others because we are locked into redundant ways of thinking. A different perspective is needed.

Let us now return to the mass in the basilica at Vézelay with which this chapter began. It began, you will recall, with the words of the priest, 'God calls. He calls always. His call is personal and universal.' They were words which seemed to come from somewhere else, from outside of the church, from deep within the being of the worshippers, from another place. The space and light, the clarity and simplicity of the music, the silences all embodied the space in the human person which was waiting to hear this word out of silence, the call of God, and waited to respond in an answering cry, 'I hear you even though I see you not . . .' Here the fragmented empty postmodern person was being addressed. That community had recognized that they had to speak of God in a different way in order to speak to those who were before them in a manner which could be heard. Repeating the old rationalist faith would no longer suffice. As I said earlier, the real question is whether we can see that our present condition, which we believe to be an affliction, is actually a gift, a moment in which we can rediscover our capacity to see and respond to the immensity of God. In the apparent emptiness of the present God calls and asks us to listen. A word emerges out of the silence. It is a call to wakefulness.

The issue will be resolved by understanding the nothingness with which we are now faced. Is this actually nothing or is it a gift which for some reason we cannot receive? This question is one which faces both the disenchanted individual in a poverty stricken part of Europe or America, faced perhaps with the question of whether they will use drugs or not, and also the great philosophers of the day. What does this silence mean? This is the question to which a large number of philosophers and theologians, many of them happily accepting the term 'postmodern', others not so happy with that term, have given their attention over the past years. The question is tackled most directly in an essay by Denys Turner. The essay was originally a sermon preached while he was Norris Hulse Professor of Divinity in Cambridge University. In this essay Turner talks of the nihilistic mentality of the postmodern person who sees nothing as real. He says,

> There is, apparently, little enough to distinguish this mentality from the Christian perception that all things are created ex nihilo, and so, in a sense for the Christian too there is only 'nothing' on the other side of 'everything'. Except this difference which is the whole difference: that for the postmodern, the world is simply given; for the Christian, the world is simply gift. The Christian and the postmodern are inversions of one another. The mirror image of 'nothing' accounting for things is love accounting for things. Both see the world as equally 'gratuitous', but in opposed senses.[10]

He elaborates this insight by recounting how he found himself, rather unwillingly, reading the German philosopher Heidegger and during his reading remarked upon his distinction between beings and their ground. This, he said, reminded him of the work of St Bonaventure who said that we only know things because they exist within the divine illumination. Bonaventure, says Turner, asserts that it is 'the invisibility of the divine light which is the cause of the visibility of creatures, and so appears to us as if the "darkness of God"'. Turner then goes on to say that while he was reminded of Bonaventure, Heidegger himself was explicitly influenced by another premodern Christian thinker, Meister Eckhart. Eckhart it is who tells us that the ground of our selfhood is the divine ground, so that, as Turner says, 'our centre is outside us, we are "decentred" beings'. The language of both Bonaventure and Eckhart is remarkably postmodern, for it is postmodern philosophers who use the language of darkness and decentring. So what strikes Professor Turner is that there are what he calls 'symmetries' between the premodern views of Bonaventure and Eckhart and the postmodern views of Heidegger and Derrida, particularly over the distinction between creatures and their ground; but it will be the theme of this book that these symmetries are far more widespread than Turner's essay suggests and that it would very much behove the postmodern cynic to look again at what he believes to be mere emptiness and push through that emptiness into the fullness of God; or, as Turner puts it, to push through what is 'simply given' to discover that all things are 'simply gift'. He says,

> the light in which the Christian sees revises the gratuity of things as grace, it reframes postmodern arbitrariness as the giftedness of all things – for since nothing requires that there should be anything at all, that there is what there is seems now to be willed, to have the inexplicability of an unknowable, creative love.[11]

Above all, the postmodern condition is one in which we can rediscover that all things are simply gift, coming from the hand of the invisible giver who is God. This realization then enables us to live entirely freely within the postmodern age and to live without fear. At this point we forget ourselves and are truly awake.

2

Meister Eckhart and the negative way

Imagine yourself in Paris in the early summer of 1310. Paris at this time had become the intellectual centre of western Christianity. Here the latest intellectual developments were debated, here the greatest thinkers of the Church, people like Albertus Magnus and Thomas Aquinas, were or had been at work. Theological debate was bread and butter for the people of Paris, and the great affair of the summer of 1310 was the trial of a woman for heresy. Debate about the place of women in the Church was commonplace. Paris, like so many of the cities of Europe, would have discussed the place of women in the Church, and whether and how they could speak or write about God, for some time. But women and their ideas plainly worried the authorities, for some years before, a noted Paris theologian, Henry of Ghent, had written about whether a woman could be a doctor of theology, and had concluded that it was impossible. The particular woman on trial in 1310 had, it was said, pushed the boundaries too far, hence a trial for heresy. One difficulty was that she was not a member of a recognized religious order, nor was she attached to the Franciscans or the Dominican 'Third Orders'. She was what was known as a Beguine, a woman who attempted to live a life of simplicity and chastity and service, after the inspiration of the Gospels. Many of them lived together in simple groups sharing a common life and were devoted to prayer and the service of the poor. Some of them wrote of the spiritual life. These women were not

19

a new phenomenon. About sixty years earlier Matthew Paris, an English Benedictine, had written about them. He said,

> At this time, especially in Germany, people of both sexes, but chiefly women, have called themselves 'religious' and have adopted a religious profession, though a light one. They take private vows of celibacy and simplicity of life, though they don't follow the rule of any saint, nor submit to enclosure. Their number has increased so much in a brief time that two thousand or more are found in Cologne and the neighbouring areas.[1]

Such women were worrying to the authorities because they were not controlled; there was no great religious order to which they were accountable. They might come out with ideas or writings which nobody had checked. This also meant that such women were very vulnerable. They were subject to theological suspicion and had no one to protect them when they became a challenge to received ideas. What disturbed the theologians of the day about the Beguines was what was considered to be a dangerous emphasis on the inner promptings of the Spirit. This could lead people into asserting that they were established in what was known as 'the liberty of the Spirit' and so had no need to obey their ecclesiastical superiors. One Henry of Freimar or Henry of Germany was particularly disturbed by these developments, and he condemned those who believed they were 'perfect and established in a liberty of the Spirit', and it must be said that he voiced the sentiments of much orthodox opinion at the time.

The woman who was on trial in Paris was intelligent and well read and had taken up a teaching role within the communities of women with which she was associated and had written a theological book. This book had been publicly condemned as heretical and burned in Valenciennes by the local bishop. But she had not been willing to be silenced, had continued to disseminate her teaching and had sought approval for her work from representatives of the religious orders and a scholastic theologian. But to no avail. In 1309 this disobedient and heretical woman was brought before the Pope's Inquisitor General in France, William of Paris. Her trial involved 21 theologians and she was condemned as a 'relapsed heretic' and burned alive in the Place de Grève on 1 June 1310. The crowds, we are told, were moved to tears of compassion by the sight of her nobility. Her name was Marguerite Porete and her book was called *The Mirror of Simple Souls*.

Marguerite's book reflects a number of common themes for Beguine women, themes which had already appeared in the work of other Beguine writers. These are themes of the centrality of love and suffering and the replacement of reason with love in the centre of the soul. Where Marguerite differs from her Beguine predecessors is her development of the themes of annihilation, what she calls the *anéantissement*, of the soul in God. This decentring of the self is, she claims, liberating. In this *néant*, this nothingness, the soul is at peace, for there it claims nothing for itself. She says,

> Thus, the soul wills nothing, says Love, since she is free; for one is not free who wills something by the will within him, what- ever he might will. For when one is a servant of oneself, one wills that God accomplish His will to one's own honour . . . To such a one, says Love, God refuses his kingdom.[2]

This 'nothingness' is where all self is abandoned so that the life of God may replace it. This is where freedom is found and the Trinitarian life of God flourishes. For the inquisitors, however, such sentiments were unacceptable. They were evidence of an attempt to claim a form of divinity for the life of the soul which might free the soul from the life of the Church and the author- ity of its teaching and could not pass. So Marguerite was burned.

The next year, 1311, another theologian was posted to Paris, one who had not been involved in her trial, but who had been there before. He returned to teach theology at the univer- sity and, as a Dominican, lodged in the Dominican house in

St Jacques where another Dominican was living, namely William of Paris, who had led the inquiry into Marguerite Porete and had condemned her to be burned. Of course they would have conversed about Marguerite. Of course the new Regius Professor, one now known as Meister Eckhart, would have been acquainted with the ideas she had put forward so persistently, and had probably read her book. As we shall see, this Meister Eckhart himself puts forward ideas which are remarkably similar to those of Marguerite Porete and he himself was condemned for heresy and tragically died as the promulgation was being made some twenty years later in 1329.

Meister Eckhart is usually assumed to be a mystic, and so, in one sense, he was, but the modern popular understanding often assumes that mystics are solitary and consumed by an attempt to unite their souls with God. But a brief glimpse into the context of Eckhart's life shows him at the very centre of ecclesiastical affairs of his day arguing his way through the University of Paris as one its great teachers and engaging in real dialogue with the currents of opinion swirling around the Europe of his day. Above all he knew what had been said, especially what the Fathers of the Church had said, about the relationship between the soul and God. He was aware of what was being said on that subject by his contemporaries, and not just those within the Christian fold, but those from other faiths, Maimonides and Avicenna in particular, whose work was particularly influential upon the Christian teachers of the time. Moreover, his experience of church life in Europe was considerable. He had served the Dominican order well in a number of administrative posts in Germany and had already taught in Paris. Nor was Eckhart's encounter with the aftermath of the burning of Marguerite Porete his only contact with the world of the Beguines. The year 1314 saw him in Strasbourg preaching to convents of Dominican nuns and to the Beguines there. Later he is in Cologne, and it is from this period that so many of his German sermons come, sermons preached to groups of women, sometimes Beguine, sometimes Dominican. It should be remembered that since 1267, forty years before Eckhart's move to Strasbourg, it had been agreed that the Dominican order should accept responsibility for women's religious houses and offer them a degree of pastoral care. Eckhart was part of all this and it is clear that his responsibilities involved talking with and preaching to the spiritual world of the women of his day. Moreover, all this occurred within the context of intense discussion within the Church of the more general question of how theology should be done. Some were deeply concerned at the spread of heresy in the Church and the bitter strife there was over authority and ascribed these difficulties to the influence of new thinking, a new intellectualism as they saw it, fuelled by Greek, Hebrew and Arabic sources. Both Eckhart and Aquinas used the work of Moses Maimonides the great Jewish writer, and Eckhart was deeply fascinated by the Persian thinker Avicenna. Eckhart and Aquinas were therefore at the cutting edge of a greater openness in Christian thinking and both were subject to attacks on their expression of the faith which in Eckhart's case proved fatal.

Eckhart's 'mysticism' must therefore been seen within this context. Here was no recluse seeking isolation from the hurly-burly of the Church. Here rather was a working theologian, a teacher and an administrator, someone attempting to find a way of expressing the faith which was both true to the tradition but also true to the experience of those whom he taught. Here was someone who had to grapple with popular expressions of the faith. Here is someone for whom the dialogue between himself and his hearers became so intense that for the authorities he was eventually deemed to have moved far too close to the position of those whom he should have been correcting. As one contemporary scholar puts it, 'Eckhart was placed in a position of administrative and theological control over nuns and other women, but rather than controlling the powerful currents of late thirteenth-century women's spirituality, he was part of them'.[3] This is why the great medieval scholar Bernard McGinn places him firmly in what he calls a third strand of medieval theological thinking, which is 'vernacular' theology. This strand, as opposed to the scholastic theology of Bonaventure and Aquinas and the monastic theology of Bernard and the Cistercians, is a theology written not in Latin but in the vernacular, and its principal exponents are a number of Beguine writers such as Marguerite Porete and Mechthild of Magdeburg and, of course, Meister Eckhart. McGinn says,

> Both Eckhart and the Beguines spoke to a new and poten-tially wider audience than the monastic mystics of the early Middle Ages. The Dominican's preaching in the vernacular is one of the most significant witnesses to the new 'democratis-ing' trend in mystical teaching evident in the thirteenth century. Eckhart preached the possibility of a radical new awareness of God, in rich and often difficult terms, not to the clerical elite of the schools, but to women and men of every walk of life. Finding one's ground in the depths of the Godhead did not require adopting a traditional religious way of life, especially not one that involved fleeing from the world. As Eckhart once put it:
>
> > When people think they are acquiring more of God in inwardness, in devotion, in sweetness, and in various approaches than they do by the fireside or in the stable, you are acting just as if you took God and muffled his head up in a cloak and pushed him under a bench. Whoever is seeking God by ways is finding ways and losing God, who in ways is hidden.
>
> Eckhart's public preaching of this radical message that per-fection was possible within the secular realm did not please everyone.[4]

Evidently not, for in the Bull of Condemnation in 1329 Eckhart is taken to task specifically for putting things 'especially before the uneducated crowd in his sermons'.

This should not lead us to suppose that everything the women of his day thought to be good was also considered good by Eckhart. There are considerable differences, particularly on the question of the validity or importance of visionary experiences and the centrality of love. As we shall see, for Eckhart detachment is more important than love. Where he and Marguerite Porete are at one, however, is in their insistence on the importance of moving into a deeper or further understanding of the union between God and the soul, a union which Porete called *anéantissement* and which Eckhart calls 'union without difference'. Here they are as one, and it was here that they both came undone before the authorities, but in order to understand what they were talking about we have to step back for a moment and try to see a little more clearly just what was happening in theological exploration at the time.

As we have already seen, at the time of Eckhart European Christendom was struggling to come to terms with Greek thought especially as found in both Aristotle and Plato. Partly this thinking was being brought to Europe and its theologians through the work of Jewish and Arabic thinkers such as Maimonides and Avicenna, whose commentaries on the Greek philosophers had spread from places of learning like Cordoba, which were under Muslim control. But however this thinking arrived in Europe, one of the central questions for Eckhart and his contemporaries was, 'What does "made in the image of God" mean?' We have to remember that all Europe at this time, whether under Christendom or under Islamic control, was fascinated by the human person. There was abroad a form of religious humanism which had different expressions, but everybody was really discovering or trying to discover what the links were between the human and the divine. How did the two relate? Hence the question, 'What did "image" mean?'

In Hebrew and Early Christian thought there were various understandings of what this 'image' was. It was patience or it was immortality of the soul. Augustine linked three parts of human consciousness – memory, understanding and the will – to the three persons of the Trinity and said that these three parts of our consciousness were traces, in Latin *vestigia*, of the Godhead within us. Others said that the image of God resided in our capacity to love God as he has loved us. In Greek thought however there is a different emphasis. For the Greek philosophers the 'image of God' resides in the 'active intellect' or in the 'divine spark' which we each possess. Albertus Magnus, the teacher whom both Aquinas and Eckhart revered, struggled to translate Greek thinking into the theological thinking of the Church and proposed that the essential property of human nature was what he called 'intellect'. The meaning of this term has narrowed considerably since the Middle Ages and it corresponds much more nearly to our contemporary term 'consciousness' than to the now narrowly rationalistic word 'intellect'. Albert and those who followed him did not use the word in the narrowly intellectual meaning that it has acquired today. This 'intellect' or 'consciousness' was, said Albert, activated by the object of its knowledge who was, of course, God, who is ever conscious. Moreover for Albert, in common with a large number of Christian writers both before and since, there were degrees of 'knowing' until the 'intellect' fuses with the source of its intelligibility, God. All this was taken up in different ways by Thomas Aquinas and then by Eckhart. For them the image of God is found in our 'active intellect' or 'the soul's spark'. Eckhart says,

> When we turn away from ourselves and from all created things, to that extent we are united and sanctified in the soul's spark, which is untouched by either space or time. This spark is opposed to all creatures and desires nothing but God, naked, just as he is in himself.[5]

This is a particularly Eckhartian expression of the relationship between God and the soul, for it is clear not only that there is an intense relationship, but that this is also one where we are 'united' and 'untouched by either space or time'. The divine spark is opposed to all that is creaturely and desires God 'naked'. This use of the term 'naked' and the sense of untouchability is a form of expression which Eckhart shares with the Beguine writers, especially Marguerite Porete and Mechthild of Magdeburg. It is also at this point that we can realize how much Eckhart's thinking looks back to an earlier mystic writer Denys the Areopagite, now better known as the Pseudo-Denys, who said that the end of human existence was 'divinization'. Denys had written in the late fifth or early sixth century. He was clear that the goal of all things is union with God. Human beings can move towards God through the threefold process of purification, illumination and then union when they attain what he calls 'divinization'. Denys's work had a profound impact upon the development of Christian spiritual thinking in the Middle Ages and it is plain that Marguerite Porete and Mechthild of Magdeburg as well as Eckhart were deeply influenced by him.

But there is more to it than the simple influence of one man's thinking. Eckhart's expression of his thinking comes out of the crucible of medieval debate about how to talk about God and how to describe the way in which God and humanity relate. Some medieval scholastic theologians had come to the view that there is an intrinsic relationship between God and the created order which was best described by means of analogy, namely that there is an analogous relationship between, say, our goodness or our wisdom and the goodness or wisdom of God. The prime expositor of this analogous way of talking about God was Thomas Aquinas. Eckhart also talks about analogy but in a very different way. He says that whatever analogy there is between us and God cannot be based upon a direct analogy as if humanity and God were of the same being. In Aquinas the analogy between God's goodness and ours is really a sort of cause and effect, a relationship in which the intrinsic goodness of things is guaranteed. Goodness is a clear gift. But in Eckhart analogy is only by imputation. We are only *lent* goodness and without

27

that goodness we are nothing. God is certainly good but we are only partially so and only in so far as God acts in us. Ultimately the goodness is not ours but God's. In other words Eckhart refuses a direct analogy of being between ourselves and God such as is proposed by Aquinas. He says,

> God does not give creatures any goodness,
> but he lends it to them.[6]

The reason this is important is that it demonstrates something of the distinctiveness between creatures and God that Eckhart believed in. God is not the same kind of being as we are. He is totally other. There can be no direct analogy of being, what the medievals call an *analogia entis*, because humanity and God are not the same kind of beings.

This can be further illuminated by looking at what Eckhart said about the being of God. For Eckhart only God is 'pure being', everything else is 'being something', 'being this or that', what philosophers call contingent being. But while God is total purity of being, intellect or consciousness, from our point of view this fullness of being cannot be determined or quantified or described as if we could see it directly. Human beings cannot see God directly. If that is the case then direct description is impossible and God cannot properly be talked about as if he were something we could see or hold, however great or magnificent he might be. Indeed there are great risks for Eckhart in only using positive or direct descriptions of God. For us God is not a thing that can be described as if he were some other thing. He is not a thing, so besides possessing fullness of being or being 'pure' being, he is also absolute nothingness because he is not a thing, certainly not a thing like us. So God is nothingness in the sense of being 'no-thing-ness'. You have to say you know nothing about God in order to keep him from being reduced to less than what he is. Oliver Davies explains this by saying that when Eckhart uses the term 'being' to describe God's nature this is only as it were from the outside. Being reveals God's existence to the creature. But once the soul has risen to be in God then the term 'being' becomes redundant. Here God is a form of emptiness or desert or nothingness. So the term 'being' is 'the garment which God wears and which simultaneously reveals and conceals him; it is the "forecourt" to the "sanctuary" in which God dwells'.[7]

In other words talking about God in terms of his 'being' alone is not enough; 'being' is not finally definitive. It might be a way into understanding him but it might also be inadequate, not enough to describe him fully. This is really a more subtle and dynamic way of looking at God than many of the theologians of his day had conceived. This is why negative language moves to the fore in Eckhart's vocabulary about God and provides another reason why simple analogies of being are, for Eckhart, inadequate.

So this little trip into the complexities of medieval scholastic theology is already beginning to show us that for Eckhart the relationship between God and the human person is a more subtle and dynamic one than that described by many others because for him the concept of the 'being' of God was something that implies we know more about God than we actually do. For Eckhart God seems to be a much more immense reality, he is beyond 'being'. Moreover in Eckhart's view it is not just God who is difficult to describe, it is also us and the human person. Our 'being' is not a static reality either, in a real sense it is not 'ours' but God's. We are not in complete possession of ourselves. As we said earlier human beings are contingent beings, like everything else that is not God. Contingent being is totally dependent upon the being of another and may, indeed could, fall out of 'being' at any moment if the source of its being so determined. It does not have any 'being' of its own. We are therefore dependent for our reality upon God. But whereas human beings are contingent they do have a greater depth, a clear capacity to enter into the depths of their own being, what we might call a greater potentiality, than other creatures. In modern language this is because the human person seems to Eckhart to be much more 'unfinished' than for many other thinkers of his day. This unfinished quality, this greater capacity for depth, this greater potentiality is also a greater openness to the transcendent and it is precisely this that leads Eckhart and indeed many of the Beguine writers, to posit a much more controversial but in the end extraordinarily powerful relationship between God and the human person than many others were prepared to countenance. It is this powerful relationship which got Eckhart into trouble just as it had done for poor Marguerite Porete.

What Eckhart proposes is that the relationship between the soul and God is best described by saying that they have a common 'ground'. This is not a relationship of being but something quite different. God is the 'ground' of the human soul. This unusual term is used by Hadewijch, one of the Beguine writers, and can be compared to Marguerite Porete's phrase, 'innermost of the soul' or 'the abyss' or what she calls 'le néant'. The important point is that this use of the term 'ground' and Eckhart's view that God was the ground of the soul took talk about the relationship between God and the soul a step further than the Christian tradition was used to, certainly further than Augustine or even Bernard of Clairvaux allowed. For them, in the union of God with the soul the substance of the human person remained intact, as we would say today, our 'identity' was preserved, but in Eckhart the soul is as it were subsumed into God so that God and the soul have a common 'ground'. He says,

> Now know, all our perfection and our holiness rests in this: that a person must penetrate and transcend everything created and temporal and all being and go into the ground that has no ground. We pray our dear Lord God that we may become one and indwelling, and may God help us into the same ground. Amen.[8]

Elsewhere he says that the spark of the soul

wants to go into the simple ground, into the quiet desert, into which distinction never gazed, not the Father, not the Son, nor the Holy Spirit. . . . For this ground is a simple silence, in itself immovable, and by this immovability all things are moved, all life is received . . .⁹

Eckhart is here describing a form of affinity between the two unknowns, the unknown because unseen nature of God and the unknown nature of the human soul. These two unknowns are in relationship. When we experience the unknown or the unfinished in ourselves then we are led to the gateway through which we may pass into the unknown of God. This might be better understood if we used another image which is implicit in Eckhart's writing on this subject and said that for Eckhart the soul was a sort of womb. He believed that all things were created through the Son, the eternal word of God and that the soul is that which bears the creative word within us, the womb within which the word is born. This means that the soul is the birthplace of the eternal in each person. In God there is a similar fecundity, he is the one who is perpetually fecund and constantly speaking his word, constantly giving birth to creatures. There is therefore a fecundity both in God and in the human soul. This fecundity – which Eckhart also calls 'nothingness' or 'wilderness' because it is beyond human knowing and opens us to the God we cannot know – is something in the soul which exists beyond mere being in the world and is in direct continuity with God. This 'fecundity' is free from the 'here and now' and has nothing in common with anything else and so can be called 'nothing'. He says,

In created things – as I have said before – there is no truth. There is something that transcends the created being of the soul, not in contact with created things, which are nothing; not even an angel has it, though he has a clear being that is pure and extensive; even that does not touch it. It is akin to the nature of deity, it is one in itself, and has naught in common with anything. It is a stumbling block to many a learned cleric. It is

31

a strange and desert place, and it is rather nameless than possessed of a name, and is more unknown than it is known.[10]

In another sermon he says,

This is what the text means 'God has sent his only begotten son into the world'. You must not by this understand the external world in which the Son ate and drank with us, but understand it to apply to the inner world. As truly as the Father in his simple nature gives his Son birth naturally, so truly does he give him birth in the most inward part of the spirit, and that is the inner world. Here God's ground is my ground, and my ground is God's ground.[11]

Although it is often expressed in negative language, really Eckhart's thinking about the relationship between us and God is very fertile. Behind his sometimes technical language, or what might appear technical or medieval to us, is not just a very fertile imagination, an imagination which pushes traditional teaching to its limits, but also a very fertile teaching in the sense that he understands the relationship between God and the soul in dynamic, fertile terms rather than in static ones. In contemporary language we would call his teaching psychologically dynamic because he sees the soul as a place of potential for growth into God provided that you keep the sense of unknowing alive in you. In one place Eckhart uses this more dynamic language when he says that God pours his life into things because he cannot but 'boil over'. His nature is 'seething' (he uses the Latin term *ebullitio* which really means 'boiling over') to create and there is a place in us in which his creativity directly comes to birth. This is a place which we do not understand, indeed cannot understand and should not understand but which is nonetheless that fertile emptiness within us which is God. We do not, as a matter of course, possess some sort of soul which is made of the same stuff as God's soul, what we possess is the potentiality to allow our selfhood to be put to one side so that we can discover the absolute nothingness, which is also the total and constant fertile creativity, of God.

What we cannot do, Eckhart insists, is to capture this and keep it as our own. This is why, when he talks about God's goodness, he says it is only 'lent' to us. It is not our possession. We cannot possess God's nature. Indeed it is at this point that Eckhart parts company with many of the Beguine writers of his day and criticizes quite sharply their expression of the relationship between God and the soul. It is also at this point that he parts company with the women in his spiritual charge who were keen to experience God as if he were their own. This is also why Eckhart praises detachment as being above love. This is certainly strange to modern ears which are so much the heirs of the tradition of romantic love. For us detachment is a coldness, and love brings us nearer to each other and to God. It should also be pointed out that such an emphasis was strange to many of his hearers. It would certainly have been strange to Julian of Norwich, whom we shall consider in our next chapter, and to the author of the English mystical treatise *The Cloud of Unknowing*, for both of those writers saw love as central in their scheme of things. It would have been foreign to most of the women, the Dominican sisters and the Beguines, to whom Eckhart was preaching. Their theology was visionary, christocentric and preoccupied with the terminology and high emotions of courtly love. What they were looking for was an intense inner experience of spiritual union with God. What they were given by Eckhart was something else, talk of 'nothingness' and nakedness and detachment. Eckhart wanted to keep the inner eyes of his hearers totally clean, he wanted them to focus on the final reality of God, which he saw as finally unknown and only really accessible through an awareness of the unknown in the self, so he praises detachment above all love because love risks descending into a form of possessiveness which makes God into an object of our own possession rather than allowing him to exist in all his wondrous unknownness. Possessiveness is consuming and pandemic, it can subvert love and make all objects of love into objects of possession, as if the lover were a tourist capturing everything with his camera ready to be kept and pored over as part of his treasury. The exercise of detachment restores our desire for God to its proper place so that it becomes an expression of contemplative reverence for creation within which God is hidden. Detachment prevents love from believing that it is the owner of the self. To use modern language once again, love without this detachment falls into the clutches of our own ego-need. Indeed, says Eckhart, the God of our own desire is a form of ego-need, and becomes a tyrant.

> Whoever now wishes to see properly what is the excellence and the profit of perfect detachment, let him take good heed of Christ's words, when he spoke about his human nature and said to his disciples, 'It is expedient for you that I go from you, for if I do not go, the Holy Spirit cannot come to you'. This is just as if he were to say: 'You have taken too much delight in my present image, so that the perfect delight of the Holy Spirit cannot be yours. So detach yourselves from the image, and unite yourselves to the formless being, for God's spiritual consolation is delicate; therefore he will not offer it to anyone except to him who disdains bodily consolations.'[12]

This is classic Eckhart teaching, and it brings us to precisely what is important about him for his contemporaries and for us.

* * * * * * * * * *

As we have seen there are a number of similarities between the theological language of some of the Beguine writers of Eckhart's day and that of Meister Eckhart. Mechthild of Magdeburg uses the same language of 'nakedness' and 'stripping' that Eckhart uses. They share a common theme of metaphysical poverty. But Eckhart's sermons, his German sermons in particular, are also a critique of the 'experientialist' theology of the Beguines, especially on the theme of 'knowing' God.

Eckhart makes it clear that you cannot 'know' God in the way you think you can. Today's preaching context is very similar to that of Meister Eckhart. The 'experientialism' of the Beguines is very similar to the experientialist theologies of today. Today large parts of the Christian Church, including the more institutionalized parts, have adopted a popular theological expression in which God is experienced through Jesus and where there is a search for a personal experience of the love of Jesus which can be called my own, my own experience of God's love in Christ. This intense 'experientialism' needs to be both understood and corrected by those in positions of theological leadership, and it is a reading of Meister Eckhart which will enlighten and inform them. Just as Eckhart listened in the fourteenth century so the Church today needs where possible to listen to and to use the same language as those who adopt an experience-based theology, but also to do as he did and seriously question this theology when it claims a direct knowledge of God. So for the simple reason that Eckhart lived and taught at a time when the religious climate was in some ways similar to our own he can be seen as a model of how to do theology in a way which preserves the reality of God from its current shallow despoilers.

But there is more to Eckhart than that. What is becoming clear now is that today's 'postmodern' context gives permission for the rediscovery of some of Eckhart's key concepts. Indeed a number of postmodern theologians have already found inspiration in his writing. Don Cupitt, in a seminal but often wrong-headed book entitled *Mysticism after Modernity*, sees Eckhart and the writers of the Dionysian mystical tradition as the precursors of a contemporary postmodern deconstructionist theology. He says,

> because mystical writing, especially in the hands of a very great figure such as Eckhart, tends to deconstruct the official church ontology, it may be seen as anticipating more recent styles of deconstructive criticism and radical theology. And if even classical mysticism was already tending to undermine

35

metaphysics . . . I can claim that our postmodern mysticism of secondariness is the true continuator of the older tradition.[13]

Cupitt's claim that Eckhart should not be dragged back into orthodoxy would hardly be recognized by Eckhart himself, but Cupitt's broader point holds good, that the present climate is one in which we can rediscover the relevance of some of Eckhart's assumptions and bring them into the service of theology today and so bring theological thinking closer to the people of the postmodern era. In particular Eckhart's understanding of the dissolution of the self in God is a strikingly familiar concept to postmodern theologians as we have already seen. Whereas for Emmanuel Levinas art turned the sovereign ego out of its house, for Eckhart it is God who does this. Eckhart is at one with postmodernism in calling for the dissolution of the 'self', but along with Christian postmodernists would see this as dissolution into God, while atheist postmodernists would see this simply as dissolution. Eckhart's view of God as beyond human 'knowing' and his subsequent affirmation of the need to live 'without a why', in simple gratuitousness, accepting the life of the universe and the self as the given outpouring of God's life, are again themes of the postmodern world, but firmly place that postmodern world within a theological framework. The atheist postmodern person lives without a why because the universe is inexplicable. Eckhart urges his Christian hearers to live without a why because the universe is within the gratuitous outpouring of God's constant spokenness.

The common denominator between the world of Eckhart and our own is that 'religion' is just as much a problem today as it was then. Eckhart urged his hearers to adopt a life of spiritual poverty. It is certainly true that a rediscovery of 'spiritual poverty' by people of faith today would go a long way to challenge those who believe that the Church is spiritually bankrupt because it is full of people who are in it for their own 'spiritual fulfilment'. Too much church life today is seen as a form of self-indulgence by those who refuse to adopt any of its beliefs or practices. Sadly these critics are too often correct in their analysis, and the Church does contain too many who are seeking a form of fulfilment which is no more than a spiritual version of the fulfilment promised by the modern world to those who would become materially or physically successful. This is no more than a form of religious capitalism which is a long way from the spiritual stripping called for in the Gospels. Eckhart's call to spiritual poverty is, therefore, enormously relevant to the contemporary Church. To classify him as a 'mystic' is actually something which prevents his message being heard because mysticism itself is regarded as a form of self-indulgence by those who do not understand its true meaning in the Christian tradition. Some would say that the Church has called him a mystic in order to protect itself from the radical and subversive nature of his teaching. But the main point is that Eckhart's teaching about the need for spiritual poverty reminds us, living as we do in an age when there are vast disparities between rich and poor, that spiritual poverty is necessary for those who would properly serve the poor. No poor person will be properly served by one who is merely searching for his own self-fulfilment in what he does, however apparently effective that service is. As Professor Denys Turner says,

> Spiritual poverty as a personal lifestyle sets us apart from the consumerism of a capitalist mentality. Without that poverty of spirit it is impossible for any person, as Eckhart says, to love God, neighbour or creation except in blasphemous idolatry. That is why it is only the poor in spirit who can do justice to the poor.[14]

It is important to close this section on the work of Meister Eckhart and his relevance to the postmodern world in which we live with some general comments on the nature of mysticism and its place within the life of the Church today. First, it cannot be overemphasized that Eckhart's language about

37

God – 'emptiness', 'nothingness', 'wilderness', 'desert', 'simple silence', 'darkness' – is language about a reality which is beyond the capacity of language to comprehend or contain. This has become known as the negative mystical way, as opposed to the affirmative way which is to be found, for example, in Bernard of Clairvaux and, as we shall see, in Thomas Traherne, the seventeenth-century English poet and writer. Looking carefully at Eckhart's language we can perhaps see that the negative way is not a denial of God's existence but a way of talking about God as if he really is God and not simply as if he were a being bigger than or greater than any other being but still another being. God is 'who he is', radically other. Negative language faces the reality of this radically other God and allows language to break down in the face of that reality. The further implication of this is that the negative way is, therefore, not a dark night of the soul in the sense of being psychologically or religiously 'lost'; which is how many contemporary writers interpret it. Such writers are trying to claim the negative way as some sort of antecedent or model for contemporary spiritual malaise and the deep sense of alienation which pervades people today. This is really a false move. Although some of the symptoms might feel the same, ultimately it cannot be compared to conditions of depression or loss of faith. It is rather a loss of ability to speak in the face of the immensity and otherness of God. It also recognizes the loss of a sense of 'self' as being ultimately beneficial, which is hardly the case for those who sense their alienation from all things.

Nor is the negative mystical way alien to a biblical faith. There is clear biblical support for talking about the 'absence' of God. In Exodus 20 Moses is called up the mountain and God tells him that he may not see his face. 'Thick darkness' is said to cover the reality of God and God's 'glory' is denied to Moses. And it is perhaps worth mentioning that the Fathers of the Church, especially Gregory of Nyssa in his important work *The Life of*

Moses, saw Moses as a basic 'type' of Christian traveller, who having lived long in the service of God in Egypt and followed his ways in tribulation and struggle, having gone through baptism in the Red Sea and been given the bread of heaven in the manna in the wilderness, is eventually brought to the dark place on the mountain where God dwells. This journey into darkness was seen by Gregory as standard for those engaged upon the Christian faith rather than exceptional. Nor, as Isaiah's comment 'verily thou art a God that hidest thyself' reveals, is the account of Moses' encounter with the thick darkness which surrounds God the only place in Scripture where negative language about God is to be found.

Contemporary accounts of the negative mystical way also often misunderstand the nature of the darkness which is experienced. A little reflection on the nature of God's immensity should reveal that if we really wish to speak about God then there are only two courses of action open to us. One is to talk but then never to stop talking because God cannot be defined or delimited by any single set of descriptors. The other is to be cast into a dumb silence, the silence of total amazement, a form of blindedness. These two alternatives are the affirmative and the negative paths. We shall come to the affirmative way and its constant struggle to find new and more adequate metaphors for God in later chapters, but it is important to note at this stage that the negative way derives not so much from a loss of awareness of God but from an excess of awareness. It is a surfeit of awareness which blinds the senses. The darkness of God is caused by an excess of light, what St John of the Cross calls 'a ray of darkness'. It is similar in spiritual terms to the physical effect of exposing the eye to the excess of light in the approaching undimmed headlights of a car at night when the eye is forced to close but then finds a dark patch on the retina which prevents full sight. As Francis Thompson says in his poem 'The Hound of Heaven',

Is my gloom but the shade of your hand,
outstretched caressingly?

It is proximity to God that brings about a sense of absence.
But there is a real sense in which both the negative and the
affirmative ways are ways of wakefulness. They are the response of those who have woken up to the true reality of God
and who are searching for adequate ways to express this sense
of wakefulness before him.

What is clear is that contemporary Christian people do
experience God in negative terms but they lack the vocabulary
with which to express this properly and the clergy lack awareness of the importance and prevalence of the negative way and
so are helpless in the face of their people's dilemmas. We need
an Eckhart in our day who will enable people to accept that
what is happening to them is actually a true way to God and
should not be rejected as the loss or death of God within them.
Such a person will also be able to speak meaningfully to those
who are outside of the Church or who left the Church because
they have not been helped to understand the loss of God
within them as part of the negative tradition. Too many are
alienated because of the contemporary heavy emphasis on the
importance of experiencing Jesus. The implication is that this
is the only way.

There are a number of important indications or signs, many
of them written about by the negative writers themselves,
especially John of the Cross, which will help those who are actually in the midst of the negative way but who think that they
have lost their hold on God, to understand that their condition is not hopeless but actually very positive. They are nearer
to God than they think. This could be the case, for example,
for somebody whose life has grown into God over many years
but for whom this growth has apparently stopped for no reason.
This may be accompanied by constant attempts to restart the
process but to no avail. This apparently negative condition is,

provided the person's engagement in the faith has been regular and constant, more likely to be a sign that the person must move on into the negative way rather than cling to the simple doctrinaire affirmations of his or her spiritual life so far. This could also be the case for those longstanding members of the Christian faith, those who, like Moses, have been schooled in the Christian way for some time, who search for answers but for whom the more they press for answers the more intense the darkness becomes. These are people whose souls may well have already embarked upon the negative way but whose rational side is unaware of this or unable to cope with this development and so may be deeply puzzled by what is happening to them. Moreover, on this dark journey difficulties will certainly be encountered. A dilemma will be experienced over the question of progress in the Christian life, for at this point false notions of 'progress' will have to be abandoned in order to be drawn into the unknown of God. Here human measurement of spiritual progress becomes an obstacle. So desire for 'progress' in the spiritual life or in the professional ministry has to be abandoned. This is extremely difficult for people whose mentality is schooled in the idea that observable progress is a necessary part of life and especially for professional people, including these days the clergy, who have to demonstrate 'progress' to their superiors. In spiritual terms there always comes a point when *real* progress is only achieved when inordinate desire for progress is abandoned.

As the desire for humanly defined progress is abandoned, a number of other things become apparent to the soul engaged upon the negative way. The first and most important of these will be a sense of the loss or death of the self, even in relation to God. In an age when self-awareness is a primary goal for most people this is often perceived to be a spiritual disaster, and anger or fear at this loss may emerge within the soul. If not anger then passivity, the reverse of anger, may result; a passivity which is actually destructive and involves a fearful refusal to let

41

go and let God be borne in us. 'What is happening to me?' becomes the constant cry of such a soul, and constant pastoral counselling is sought. But the wise counsellor will say that this darkness does not go away – nor should it. When counselling fails then therapy is demanded to relieve the sense of spiritual darkness which has invaded the soul. The best therapists tell such a person to go on into the darkness. People in this stage of development also resist a shift in their prayer life, a shift to a more contemplative style of prayer. They want answers, and asking or talking is assumed to be the only valid form of prayer. Childhood patterns of prayer are maintained over against a desire by the inner being to move into different ways.

But adherence to the negative way brings a number of real gains to the human soul. First, a different understanding of God becomes possible, an understanding where God is the source of all being rather than simply the object of belief. A great many contemporary theological discussions could simply be avoided, dropped even, without loss if theological teachers were more aware of the importance of this shift. Far too much time is spent asking questions about how expressions of belief, usually credal expressions, can be compatible with a modern rational approach to faith. These discussions not only make a mistake about theological language, as Archbishop Rowan Williams points out in an essay on 'Theological Integrity',[15] but also make a mistake about the object of theological language, who is God. God is not there to be examined but to be known as the source of all being. This also means that the believer is the 'known' rather than the knower. The believer does not possess an overarching viewpoint, that is a chimera as far as theology is concerned. The fact that the believer is 'known' by God is, of course, the primary reason why there is so much sexual imagery in mystical texts, imagery of ravishing or yearning and why the Song of Songs was, for so long, the primary scriptural text for the mystical writers. But once the threshold of the negative way has been passed and the believer ceases to be preoccupied with truth then great strides can be made. Prayer becomes much more contemplative and profound, preoccupation with church administration becomes less central and a capacity to serve the marginalized is released from its captivity within the soul, and joy and enchantment invade the whole person. This is the wakefulness that is the true condition of the soul but which is obscured or hidden from us by our need for answers and certainties.

All this was well known to the author of *The Cloud of Unknowing*, an English mystic of the fourteenth century, who says,

> all that you find is darkness, a sort of cloud of unknowing; you cannot tell what it is, except that you experience in your will a simple reaching out to God. This darkness and cloud is always between you and your God . . . So set yourself to rest in this darkness, as long as you can, always crying out after him whom you love . . . When I say darkness I mean a privation of knowing . . .[16]

So the negative way is a form of breakdown of language in the face of the brilliance of the glory of God. It is a breakdown of the sense of self in the face of God and a reliance upon God totally for identity. Once this breakdown has occurred – and Meister Eckhart is the preacher par excellence of the need for such a breakdown – then much can occur which is otherwise locked away. At this point we truly awake.

3

Julian of Norwich and the body politic

In June 1381, exactly seventy years after the burning of Marguerite Porete for heresy in Paris, one Wat Tyler and a priest called John Ball were executed by the forces of Richard II, King of England, just outside London. Some days later all of the rest of their supporters were hunted down and executed, the last of them in Norwich. Wat Tyler had not taught any explicitly theological heresy but had led a rebellion, now known as the Peasants' Revolt, against the imposition of a flat rate poll tax in 1380. This tax had been imposed by the king's Chancellor, the Archbishop of Canterbury, Simon of Sudbury. During the rebellion Simon of Sudbury had taken refuge with the king in the Tower of London. The rebels had already taken the town of Canterbury and despoiled the Archbishop's lands. They then entered London and controlled the city for several days. Sudbury resigned the Chancellorship, but this was not enough to satisfy the rebels, and on 14 June he was captured by the mob and executed. From this point onwards the king gave no quarter and the revolt ended in an ignominious defeat and the execution of all of the leaders.

Among the peasants' demands was the complete elimination of 'villeinage', the servile status of the common person. John Ball's famous couplet illustrates their position:

> When Adam dalf, and Eve span
> Who was thanne a gentleman?

And the chronicler Froissart gives an account of Ball's preaching where

> the matters goeth not well to pass in England, nor shall do till everything be common, and that there be no villains nor gentlemen, but that we may be all united together, and that lords be no greater masters than we be.[1]

It is clear that the abolition of lordship would have resulted in a radical overturning of the social order in England and it was inevitable that this would not be allowed to pass at that time. But the peasants' revolt was not simply about the social order. It came towards the end of a century which had already seen death and tragedy on a huge scale together with enormous social upheavals. The whole century had been a difficult one and would continue to be so well after the death of Wat Tyler and his allies. There had been a series of catastrophic harvests in England, especially in 1369, which had resulted in widespread hunger and deprivation. There had been regular outbreaks of anthrax among cattle and then the plague had arrived. It came to England's shores in Dorset in August 1348, and reached London in the November of that year and the city of Norwich in January 1349. One-third of the population of Norwich died. Half of the clergy were lost before the epidemic abated. Nor had all gone well in affairs of state. Edward III had come to the throne in 1330 at a very young age partly through the intrigues of his mother. He had quarrelled with Scotland and France and invaded France in 1339. The war which followed, now known as the Hundred Years War, drained England of men and resources. It began well with victory at the Battle of Crécy in 1346, but for a long time was inconclusive and expensive to maintain.

Nor was the religious life of the nation any more settled. This was the time when there were two rival Popes, one in Rome, the other in Avignon, and Christendom was divided. Pope Urban VI in Rome began a military campaign against his rival,

Clement, in Avignon, a campaign which was led by the militaristic and influential bishop of Norwich, Henry Despenser. This campaign was defeated and many from Norwich, who had loyally followed their bishop, died in the conflict. As well as military conflict there was spiritual and theological conflict within the church. John Wycliffe (?1330–84) was teaching at Oxford where he not only made a distinction between the eternal and spiritual reality of the Church and its visible 'material' expression, but also maintained that the Bible should be the sole criterion of Christian doctrine and said that the authority of the Pope was ill-founded in Scripture as was the doctrine of transubstantiation in the Eucharist. These ideas were taken up by his followers, known as 'Lollards', who attacked ecclesiastical authority. It was among them that the first English Bible was produced in the 1390s and among them that there was a focus on devotion to Christ and his law together with the assertion that if the clergy did not live morally and spiritually according to this law then they should be deprived of their positions. In 1397 a group of English bishops, led by Henry Despenser, bishop of Norwich, requested the death penalty against Lollards, which was granted.

But Lollards were not the only source of disquiet in the Church. We have already seen the importance of the Beguine movement in the life of Meister Eckhart. Beguines flourished in the Netherlands, and the city of Norwich had grown prosperous because of its capacity for trade with the Low Countries. There Mechthild of Magdeburg and Hadewijch of Brabant had been writing, and it is inconceivable that their ideas had not crossed the North Sea and were circulating in England. Brigit of Sweden, who in many ways represents the intellectual flowering of continental European women writers of this period, did not die until 1373. In that same year in King's Lynn an English woman was born who was full of devotion to Christ and who did travel abroad and who did cause the authorities a great deal of irritation if not distinct trouble at the end of the century and during the early years of the next. Her name was Margery Kempe. She was tried for heresy in 1417, found innocent and died about 1440. Her written account[2] records her struggle to find oneness with God at a time of struggle and dislocation in society. In her difficulties she consulted another woman in East Anglia, Julian of Norwich, an anchoress whose cell was a short distance from the 'Lollard's Pit' in Norwich, where heretics were burned.

So while Wat Tyler and his friends had focused on a number of particular demands, their revolt was an indication of the enormous sense of disturbance and disquiet which was abroad in the land at this time. Some commentators have suggested that the peasants' revolt was in fact a late revolt and that a number of their demands were already redundant. Whatever truth this suggestion contains it indicates that by the end of the fourteenth century there was in England a certain loosening of social structures and a degree of uncertainty about how society should move forward which might well have enabled this revolt to take place. In the turmoil of the fourteenth century new ideas had been struggling to be born. There is no doubt that this struggle was acute. There were serious attempts by the civil and ecclesiastical authorities to keep new ideas in check, and at times those who held them were mercilessly suppressed. These ideas were, of course, ideas which today we find perfectly acceptable; ideas about the importance of good mutual relationships between the governed and those who exercise governance, ideas about the place of love and forgiveness not just between individuals but also within society. In the Church these ideas were about how the individual might experience the love of God, and how this was mediated through Christ, they were about the place of suffering and death and how the suffering and death of Christ relate to the suffering of us all. What does our suffering and death and God's love and forgiveness really mean and how can they be understood? In overall terms the real question was whether the body politic, which was not merely a secular body but one in which both church and king played a central role, could encompass these new ideas. Was the body politic merely a controlling body or could it actually embody these new ideas? In theological terms the question was how these new ideas could relate to the traditional teaching of the Church. Were these ideas such as would undermine authority, in church or state? Was the love of God central and if so how was this to be understood in a violent and controlling environment? Could the Church, could Christians, put this love into effect in life?

The interesting thing is that in various parts of Europe for the last hundred years, by and large it had been women who had thought and written about these things. The men were concerned more with the abstract debates of the theological schools. Women had often paid a very high price for thinking the unthinkable as we have seen with Marguerite Porete, but it is remarkable how, in various places, and often not very connected one with the other, women had reflected on the nature of God's love and the quest for unity in the soul and healing in society. We have already spoken of the Beguines, but before the rise of the Beguines, in the twelfth century, Hildegaard of Bingen had spoken of how human beings and the created world all rest in the womb of God, saying, 'you are encircled by the arms of the mystery of God'. She went on to push the limits of contemporary understanding about the role of women saying that in the first woman 'the whole human race was present in a latent way'. So some of the ideas of the Beguines were hardly new. In the fourteenth century Brigit of Sweden had founded a religious order for men and women in parallel monasteries originally both under the authority of an Abbess who represented Mary. In her spiritual writings Brigit, who wrote in the vernacular, saw Mary as an active partner in the redemptive ministry of Christ and spoke of the way in which she and her son shared the same heart. In all of her work Brigit aimed to give theological and spiritual validation to human femaleness in a way which was unprecedented, even in Hildegaard. So it is not surprising to find a religious Englishwoman, living in East Anglia, writing a book at this time on these topics. Nor was it surprising to find her writing in the vernacular as her sisters on the continent had done. English had now become a language of sonority and importance, increasingly used as the vehicle of both spiritual and literary reflections. The *Showings* of Julian of Norwich, the 'short text' of which dates from 1373, was therefore one of the earliest serious theological works to appear in English and Julian represents the English flowering of European women's vernacular talk about God.

Her book is a treatise on the love of God – 'Love was his meaning' – and for a number of reasons history has put Julian down as a mystic or as a spiritual writer. She has been widely adopted as a spiritual icon by many of those in our own time who have become enamoured of 'spirituality'. A woman spiritual writer, an English woman spiritual writer at that, who talks of the motherhood of God, has naturally been seized upon as an early example of what such women are doing now. She is seen as an early trailblazer – and rightly so – for the contemporary feminist movement. But there is much more to Julian than a trailblazer for contemporary feminism, and indeed much of her significance for her own time and for today will be lost if she is understood only in those terms. A warning note should be heard when it is realized that her theology is far more dense and complex than that of most of her contemporaries and often far more dense and complex than is expected or desired by contemporary readers. As Frederick Bauerschmidt says,

> Julian's popularity is a result of the variety of ways in which she is read and purposes to which she is put. Should she be read as a theologian, who can aid us in probing and expanding the Christian theological tradition? Should she be read as someone who is both a victim of and resistant to medieval misogyny, who can help us understand the status of women in medieval

society and culture? Is she a devotional writer who can help today in tending to our prayer life? These differing interests with which readers approach the text produce radically different, and at times even incommensurable, readings.[3]

However much any or all of these different readings of Julian are true none of them take seriously enough the social and political context of her writing or see her as somebody who, as Bauerschmidt says, 'theologically imagines the political'. Theology and politics have, of course, been driven apart in the twentieth century. Theology has been driven into the purely personal and emotional realms. Such a situation would have been inconceivable in Julian's day. Her themes – suffering and death, the place of God's love, the relationship between Christ and humanity and the meaning of forgiveness – are all part of both the civil and ecclesiastical fabric of her day. The important and often unrealized point is that her resolution of these themes, her way of understanding, is apparently in conflict with the teaching of the Church. Julian speaks of a God in whom there is no wrath and a Christ who dwells peaceably at the centre of the human soul; and the question which she asks at the end of the day and which today's people of faith need to ask in turn, is, 'Can the body politic, can the Church and the state, actually incorporate and so live out these realities?'

So on about 13 May 1373, the 31-year-old Norwich woman whom we now know as Julian, but whose baptismal name is lost, and who later described herself as 'a simple creature unlettyrde', received a revelation from God. She had fallen seriously ill with a life-threatening illness and after three days received the last rites. Three nights later she was thought to be near death and the local priest was called and in his ministrations to her held a crucifix before her face saying that he had brought the image of the saviour. Julian saw the crucifix begin to bleed, something which prompted a series of revelations, sixteen in all, which she described as 'a revelation of love'.

Plainly Julian recovered and wrote an account of her revelations or *Showings*. This account survives in two versions; the short text, which probably dates from 1373, the year in which Julian received her visions, and the long text, which is a more expanded account and dates probably from the 1390s. The short text is fresh and easy to read, but does not contain Julian's more mature theological reflections. The long text contains meditations on 'the godly will', the wrath, or lack of it, of God, meditations on the motherhood of God and, most importantly in view of the social context within which the book was written, the parable of the Lord and the servant. As we read the long text we realize that what had at first been an account of a set of visions, described in the conventional religious expression of the day, becomes a serious and highly wrought reflection on the whole question of how we relate to God and what or how God is towards us. And underneath it all is a serious and highly wrought argument with the received ecclesiastical wisdom of the day. Ultimately it is a call to her fellow Christians, whom she calls her 'even Christen', and through them to us, to wake up to the true reality of God and the import of that reality for the sort of lives we might live and which society might embody.

Julian's way into all this is through the vision of a bleeding crucifix. Even the mention of a bleeding crucifix to some modern minds seems primitive and somehow slightly distasteful. But modern people need to be careful before they apply modern criteria to this medieval text, or indeed apply modern views about what humanity needs to the inner authenticity of Julian and her visions. These visions and her prayers for 'three wounds' were central and real. We cannot dismiss them as 'primitive'. Nor was Julian some sort of lone mystic or visionary. She struggled with common problems and was offering her readers a way of seeing things which she believed should be 'performed' in the world. Nor is Julian's writing always easy. She and her book emerged within a particular set of circumstances: she was familiar with medieval theology and her writing is often dense and highly wrought. She is certainly not the easy writer on spirituality which the somewhat emotionalized contemporary climate looks for.

This is plain at the outset of the book. The revelations begin with a reminder of her prayer. She had been beseeching the Lord for three things: for 'the mynd of the passion'; for 'bodily sicknesse' and for 'three wounds'. These three wounds were: 'The wound of true contrition, the wound of loving compassion, and the wound of longing with my will for God.'[4] It is interesting that she asked for 'the mynd of the passion', for such a prayer is indicative of a widespread shift of attention in the devotion of Western Europe at this time. It is indicative of a shift of interest in the thirteenth and fourteenth centuries from Christ as the somewhat objective hero or the vindicator, a view associated largely with Anselm, to Christ the suffering one. This, of course, was a different piety, a more affective and loving piety where Christ the sufferer and the suffering Christian – especially, it might be said, the Christian who had suffered from the ravages of the fourteenth century – were understood as suffering together. This shift is not only evident in the literature of the time but also in the iconography, the stained glass and the paintings of Christ which this period produced. Nor was this prayer, it should be said, a plea for some sort of individual mystical ecstasy; rather Julian wanted to enter more surely into the passion of Christ and its costly transformation of her life. This was, she believed, along with so many others at this time, her only hope. There was nothing else. She also says that she asks for 'bodily sicknesse',

> Because I wanted to be purged by God's mercy and afterwards live more to his glory because of this sicknesse.

So this prayer is part of the first.

She then prays for three wounds. These were,

> The wound of true contrition, the wound of loving compassion, and the wound of longing with my will for God . . .[5]

This prayer was part of popular piety and derived from the story of St Cecilia, who died of three wounds to her neck, but it also uses a basic imagery of 'wounding' which was common in the devotional language of the Beguines. Mechthild of Magdeburg says,

> Whosoever shall be sore wounded by love
> Will never become whole
> Save he embrace the self-same love
> Which wounded him.[6]

Later in the book Julian develops the imagery of woundedness and relates it to the wounded Christ and to his wounds by which we are healed. In this way 'woundedness' mysteriously becomes the means of finding wholeness:

> When we come up and receive that sweet reward which grace has made for us, there we shall bless and thank our Lord, end-lessly rejoicing that we ever suffered woe; and that will be because of a property of the blessed love which we shall know in God, which we might never have known without woe preceding it . . .[7]

Grace Jantzen, whose study of Julian did so much to rehabilit-ate Julian as so much more than a simple devotional writer, comments on the three 'beseechings' of Julian which precipitated her visions,

> In spite of their strangeness to modern conceptions, solid commonsense pervades these prayers. Julian was not praying for visions for their own sakes, or for strange spiritual or phys-ical occurrences to gratify a religious mania. She was praying rather for greater integration, compassion and generosity; and it seemed to her that these means would enable her to develop them.[8]

But what does Julian say about the visions or revelations which she received as a result of these prayers? The first vision is of the bleeding crucifix. Her serious reflections begin at this point, for it is here that the long text begins to differ significantly from the short text. In the long text she says,

> And at this, suddenly I saw the red blood running down from under the crown, hot and flowing freely and copiously, a living stream, just as it had at the time when the crown of thorns was pressed on his blessed head. I perceived truly and powerfully, that it was he who just so, both God and man, himself suffered for me, who showed it to me without any intermediary. And in the same revelation, suddenly the Trinity filled my heart full of the greatest joy, and I understood that it will be so in heaven without end to all who will come there. For the Trinity is God, God is the Trinity. The Trinity is our maker, the Trinity is our protector, the Trinity is our everlasting lover, the Trinity is our endless joy and our bliss, by our Lord Jesus Christ and in our Lord Jesus Christ. And this was revealed in the first vision and in them all, for where Jesus appears the blessed Trinity is understood, as I see it.[9]

And then the words of the long text revert to the short text with Julian's conventional exclamation at the vision and the privilege of this vision for one such as her:

> And I said: 'Blessed be the Lord!' . . . and I was greatly astonished by this wonder and marvel, that he who is to be revered and feared would be so familiar with a sinful creature living in this wretched flesh. . . .[10]

The interesting thing is that she moves, in this later reflection, from a vision of the bleeding crucifix to a reflection upon the Trinity. We might wonder, we moderns, why she did not move into a reflection upon the crucifix as an example of the saving love of Christ? Why the Trinity rather than the atonement? That, we would think, would be more natural and right. But not so, she talks immediately about the Trinity, and a moment's reflection will enable us to see that our assumption that she should move into a reflection on the atonement at this point is really a result of our post-Reformation mentality, for it is the theologians of the Reformation who have conditioned us to think that the cross is primarily about atonement for sin. In this earlier period a different take was possible, and understanding that difference will help us to see where Julian's theology took her and where it might take us.

Julian's vision of the crucifix is her way into the immensity of God as Trinity. The cross is a pathway to or sacrament of the Trinity. Nor should we be surprised at this for it is an entirely biblical perspective. Julian is at one with the author of St John's Gospel in seeing that the life of the Trinity is apparent in the passion of Christ. This is particularly evident in the farewell discourses of Jesus, where the about-to-be-crucified Messiah speaks of the need for his disciples to abide in him as he abides in the Father. And the connection between the passion and the Godhead is made even more explicitly in the Letter to the Hebrews, where we are told,

> But when Christ had offered for all time a sacrifice for sins, 'He sat down at the right hand of God . . .'[11]

Moreover, in Julian's vision the Trinity is described in the language of total integration, as inclusive and binding all things together. 'The Trinity is our maker, protector, everlasting lover . . .' This is the complete fascination for Julian and should be for us for she looks at the passion of Jesus and sees so much more than a redeeming death. She moves into the immensity of God from the particulars of Jesus' suffering. In one sense the whole revelation of God is contained in the sight of Jesus' suffering. As Julian herself says right at the beginning of her book,

> This is a revelation of love which Jesus Christ, our endless bliss, made in sixteen showings, of which the first is about his precious crowning of thorns; and in this was contained and specified the blessed Trinity, with the incarnation and the union between God and man's soul, with many fair revelations and teachings of endless wisdom and love in which all the revelations which follow are founded and connected.[12]

Here we can see that Julian constantly probes the mystery of
the cross but finds in it mysteries which are beyond articulation. As one of our postmodern theologians has said,

> On the cross, the Word is killed, but thus is manifested, in a
> totally paradoxical light, an *other* discourse.[13]

As the book progresses Julian's articulation of the cross and
its relationship with the Trinity becomes deeper and more all-
embracing. Later in the book she does use the term 'mother'
in relation to Christ, and although she does not use that term
at the beginning, its foundation is here, for the term 'mother'
develops out of her theology of the Trinity. It is a metaphor for
the all-inclusive and enfolding love of God.

All of this is then expanded in Julian's vision of the hazelnut
which is recounted in the following chapter, chapter 5 of the
long text. She says,

> In this same time our lord shewed to me a ghostly sight of
> his homely loveing. I saw that he is to us everything that is
> good and comfortable for us. He is our clotheing that for love
> wrappith us and all beclosyth us for tender love, that hee
> may never leave us, being to us althing that is gode, as to myne
> understondyng . . .
>
> Also in this he shewed a littil thing, the quantitye of an hesil
> nutt in the palme of my hand; and it was as round as a balle.
> I lokid thereupon with eye of my understondyng and thowte:
> 'What may this be?' And it was generally answered thus: 'It is
> all that is made.' I mervellid how it might lesten, for methowte
> it might suddenly have fallen to nowte for littil. And I was
> answered in my understondying: 'It lesteth and ever shall, for
> God loveth it; and so allthing hath the being be the love of God.'[14]

I have quoted this famous passage in the original Middle
English[15] partly to show readers what the original language looks
like to our modern eyes, but mainly because of the wonderful
way in which that language speaks the sense of the text.
'Wrappith us and all beclosyth us' has far more meaning and

resonance, I think, than 'embraces us and shelters us' which is the usual modern English translation, and it shows how Julian understands that God encloses everything within his Trinitarian existence. The Trinity is not a puzzle to be understood but a mystery which envelops all things and in which we and all things live and come awake. Here there is a sense of how all things are involved in God, everything is integrated, which we shall find throughout Julian's text and which is a particular characteristic of much postmodern theological reflection. Here God is maker, lover, and preserver all together. Here we step into the terrifying passion of Christ only to find ourselves enclosed within the all-embracing love of the creator.

But the vision of the hazelnut does more than point up Julian's theology of the Trinity. It also moves us on in our understanding of God's goodness. Julian spends a moment at the end of her account drawing an analogy between the simplicity of the hazelnut, which represents 'all that is', and the simplicity of the soul which comes to God 'naked, open and familiarly', an analogy which will come to greater fruition when Julian speaks more about prayer later in the book, but then she says,

> And these words of the goodness of God are very dear to the soul, and very close to touching our Lord's will for his goodness fills all creatures and all his blessed works full, and endlessly overflows in them.[16]

It is at this point that we should pause and reflect, for here Julian is hinting at something which will take her into a difficult place. How can one who lived in the fourteenth century and had witnessed or had recounted to her all the terrible things that had happened, how could somebody who had lived through the plague say that God's goodness filled all of his blessed works? This is the first hint of her doctrine of the absence of wrath in God, but it is at first sight a very radical doctrine of the creation.

What she means becomes clear in the passages which speak of her third revelation, which begins in chapter 11 of the long text. Plainly Julian has reflected upon her original expression and found more to say. In the opening words of the book she had told us what to expect with the third revelation:

> The third revelation is that our Lord God Almighty, all wisdom and all love, just as truly as he has made everything which is, so truly he does and performs all things which are done.[17]

But in chapter 11 where she describes this revelation she adds this passage to the words of the short text,

> So I understood in this revelation of love, for know well that in our Lord's sight there is not chance; and therefore I was compelled to admit that everything which is done is well done, for our Lord does everything. For at this time the work of creatures was not revealed, but the work of our Lord God in creatures; for he is at the centre of everything, and he does everything.[18]

This picks up on and expands the significance of her words at the end of the vision of the hazelnut, where she said that God's goodness fills all his creatures. Then there is this remarkable and moving passage,

> See, I am God. See, I am in all things. See, I do all things. See, I never remove my hands from my works, nor ever shall without end. See I guide all things to the end that I ordain them for, before time began, with the same power and wisdom and love with which I made them; how should anything be amiss?[19]

This is a remarkable message of confidence in God and his continuing activity in the creation in the face of the disasters of the century. Nor is it an isolated part of Julian's thinking, for later she says, as is well known, 'All shall be well and all manner of thing shall be well.'[20] In this third revelation Julian shows that she believes that God is not just the creator, not just the sustainer, but also the constant author of all things in the present moment. This means that for her although it might appear that men or the evil one is in control, actually in and through these appearances God is doing everything and doing it well. 'How should anything be amiss?'

But this passage is much more than a remarkable affirmation in the face of death, it is also a challenge to the teaching of the Church of her day. Indeed Julian's difficulties begin at this point for she appears to adopt a radical doctrine of creation which could have been seen by the ecclesiastical authorities as a challenge to traditional teaching about human responsibility, the human capacity for sin and the subsequent judgement of God upon us. 'What about sin?' she would be asked. However, it is not until chapter 27 of the long text and revelation 13 that Julian gets round to facing this question. The chapters in between the third and the thirteenth visions contain extended reflections on the passion of Christ and then on his joy at our redemption and our joy at our awareness of that; and they enlarge our understanding of what Julian means far beyond a simple statement of the constant authorship of God in creation. For Julian all things are an expression of God's joy and our souls will feast with God in that joy. But once that has been said clearly and at some length Julian then returns to face the theological conundrum which her vision leaves. If her vision is correct then why did God allow sin in the first place?

> And so in my folly before this time I often wondered why, through the great prescient wisdom of God, the beginning of sin was not prevented. For then it seemed to me that all would have been well.[21]

Julian then goes on to give three different responses to this question which she says she has to ask but knows that the very asking of it lacks 'discretion'. First she says that sin is a necessary part of the human condition but if we bear it as such all will be well.

> Sin is necessary, but all will be well and all will be well, and every kind of thing will be well.[22]

Then she rehearses a common theological understanding of sin, one which ultimately comes from Augustine, saying that sin has no substance, is nothing of itself. As she says elsewhere, 'sin is no deed', sin is not an action which has its own integrity. Evil only exists as the shadow side of goodness.

> But I did not see sin, for I believe that it has no kind of substance, nor share in being, nor can it be recognised except by the pain caused by it.[23]

All this would have been readily understood and accepted by her contemporaries and by the ecclesiastical authorities. Where she begins to enter into difficulties is with her third response to the reality of sin which is when she says that God does not blame us for sin. The first two points are uncontroversial, but the third is difficult, for surely we are blamed for sin and sin is the cause of Christ's passion? If we are not to be blamed for sin then why was there a need for Christ to redeem us by his death? From then on Julian argues that the problem of sin is ours, not God's. The horror and danger of sin are not diminished or made light of, we are right to accept responsibility for sin and the Church is right to condemn it, but the problem is ours, *God* does not blame us for sin and continues to love us. 'Our sins are known to the Church on earth' but everything is turned to honour by God's love.

> And this is a supreme friendship of our courteous Lord, that he protects us so tenderly whilst we are in our sins; and furthermore he touches us most secretly, and shows our sins by the sweet light of mercy and grace. But when we see ourselves so foul, then we believe that God may be angry with us because of our sins. Then we are moved by the Holy Spirit through contrition to prayer, and we desire with all our might an amendment of ourselves to appease God's anger . . .

And she continues,

> . . . and then our courteous Lord shows himself to the soul, happily and with gladdest countenance, welcoming it as a friend,

61

as if it had been in pain and in prison, saying, My dear darling, I am glad that you have come to me in all your woe. I have always been with you, and now you see me loving, and we are made one in bliss. So sins are forgiven by grace and mercy, and our soul is honourably received in joy, as it will be when it comes to heaven. . . .[24]

So not only does God not blame us for our sins, however much the Church may well be right to do so, but even more remarkably there is also, in Julian's understanding of the self, a point in that self which because it wills to be saved, has never actually assented to sin. It is this reality which is called 'darling' and which she also calls 'the godly will'.

For in every soul which will be saved there is a godly will which never assents to sin and never will.[25]

In her teaching about 'the godly will' Julian shows how close she was to some of the great thinkers of the Middle Ages, especially the Cistercians, for it is William of St Thierry, a close friend of Bernard of Clairvaux, who says in *The Golden Epistle*,

For love (*amor*) is a great will toward God, another love (*dilectio*) is a clinging to him or uniting to him, and a third love (*caritas*) is delight in him. Yet the unity of the spirit with God in a man who lifts up his heart towards God is the perfection of his will, when he not only wills God's will, he is not only drawn to God, but in that drawing he is so made perfect that he can will nothing but what God wills. For to will what God wills, this is to be like God; not to be able to will except what God wills, this is to be what God is, for whom willing and being are one and the same.[26]

For William and the other medievals who followed him this thinking finds its scriptural basis in the letters of John where they read 'Beloved, we are God's children now . . . when he is revealed, we will be like him . . .'[27] And indeed such sentiments were hardly uncommon in medieval times although expressed in different ways. Eckhart, as we have seen, speaks of the 'ground of the soul' where the soul is one with God, and some time later Teresa of Avila would speak of the water of life continually springing up within the soul and relate that to the words of Jesus recounted in St John's Gospel, 'Out of the believer's heart shall flow rivers of living water.'[28] What is tragic is that this affirmative and participatory view of the relationship between the soul and God has been abandoned in our own day for a much more cynical and negative view of the self where human beings are regarded as held captive by alien forces outside of their control and so incapable of any real good. The Cistercians and Julian were greater humanists than we in our so called 'humanistic' age, claim to be.

But there is more to the notion of the godly will than agreement with the Cistercians, because for Julian it forms the basis for prayer. For Julian prayer is the expression of the soul which is united to God, it is, in fact, the life of the Trinity at work within us, it is the voice of the godly will. When she says, 'I am the ground of your beseeching'[29] she gives expression to this life.

> Prayer unites the soul to God, for though the soul may be always like God in nature and in substance restored by grace, it is often unlike him in condition, through sin on man's part. Then prayer is a witness that the soul wills as God wills, and it eases the conscience and fits man for grace.[30]

Readers of the long text of Julian's *Showings* will also realize that her understanding of the love of God and the unity of the soul in God develop as she writes. She becomes clearer and bolder about the unity between the soul and God but also clearer and bolder about the fact that God's ever-present goodness means that in God there cannot be any anger. She says,

> . . . we deserve pain, blame and wrath. And despite all this, I saw truly that our Lord was never angry, and never will be.[31]

And again,

63

Because he is God, he is good, he is truth, he is love, he is peace; and his power, his wisdom, his charity and his unity do not allow him to be angry. For I saw truly that it is against the property of his power to be angry, and against the property of his wisdom and against the property of his goodness. God is that goodness which cannot be angry, for God is nothing but goodness. Our soul is united to him who is unchangeable goodness. And between God and our soul there is neither wrath nor forgiveness in his sight . . .[32]

It is worth dwelling on this idea for a moment because it is so startling to modern ears, accustomed to wrestling with the Protestant legacy of judgement and the wrath of God. The great wonder of Julian is how clear and simple this idea is to her. The fact that it is so clear and simple gave her a degree of anxiety in view of the traditional teaching of the Church. But the statement is clear and is repeated at several points in the later part of the long text. She is sure and clear about the nature of God. God does not forgive because he cannot be angry and if there was wrath in God then we should simply not exist. Julian's dilemma is to how to reconcile what she had come to know in herself as being true about God and what the Church traditionally taught, a dilemma over which she says she 'cried within me with all my might, beseeching God for help'.[33]

The reconciliation is given to her in the wonderful parable of the Lord and the servant. This is told in the long text in chapter 51 with Julian's own comments on the parable to be found in the following chapters. The parable is both simple and complex. It tells of a Lord sitting in state who looks lovingly upon his servant and sends him on an errand. The servant is full of earnest zeal and in rushing to fulfil his Lord's command falls into a ditch and is injured to such an extent that he cannot get himself out. The servant is, moreover, unable to see how his courteous Lord stands nearby looking at him with love and pity, because he is totally focused on his own woes and difficulties. Julian then looks carefully to see if the Lord attached any blame to the servant in his situation, but found that there was none, 'for the only cause of his falling was his goodwill and his great desire'.[34]

There is a similar parable in the writings of Anselm. In his *Cur Deus Homo* Anselm tells the story of a servant who is given a task by his master who warns him about a pit that is in his way. The servant ignores the warning and throws himself into the pit and so is unable to perform his task. Anselm asks whether the servant can be excused his failing. The traditional answer is of course that he cannot be excused because the failing was his own, but this is where Julian differs from the tradition, for she says that he is not only excused but never even blamed. His fall is the result of zeal not of a rebellious will and his Lord cannot be angry because he loves his servant and constantly looks upon him with tender pity. So there is no fault in the servant and no blame is imputed to him by the Lord. '. . . the only cause of his falling was his good will and his great desire'.

The subversive and difficult nature of Julian's conclusions should not be underestimated. This is not only a totally subversive reinterpretation of the doctrine of the fall but it is also a totally subversive reinterpretation of the feudal relationship. What is plain from the parable and Julian's own comments upon it is that as Julian sees things God never looks at human beings in themselves, as isolated entities, as objectively sinning or not as the case may be. God always looks at humanity as being in Christ, for that is what is the case and has been from the beginning. From the beginning until the end God sees all of humanity as enfolded within the incarnation of Christ. This makes it very difficult for Julian to see humanity as objectively 'fallen' at one particular time because we exist within Christ at all times. There is no time when we are not in him. Traditionally speaking the fall of man was regarded as the cause of Christ's incarnation by which he effects our redemption, but for Julian this time gap is removed by the constant mutual indwelling of the Son and humanity. But Julian's description of the relationship between the Lord and the servant has further repercussions, this time for the way in which we dwell together in society. We have seen something of the difficulties which Julian's society suffered in the Peasants' Revolt and the repercussions for English society. If we read Julian's text against the background of the events of the fourteenth century as described earlier in this chapter we can see that Julian is presuming that the servant is raised by his Lord to his right hand and is clothed in new robes which indicate his status. This is not what would have happened in fourteenth-century England. As Bauerschmidt says,

> The feudal social ideal would not only take a dim view of the kind of transformation of the servant that Julian describes, but would see it as a positive threat to the divinely sanctioned order of human relations. The servant is not only made equal with the Lord, but he is clothed in a garment which is 'rychar than was the clothyying which I saw on the fader'.[35]

But Julian's radical vision is not exhausted yet. At the end of the parable of the Lord and the Servant she moves into an account of what it is that is at the bottom of the human soul. If the servant can be raised up to the right hand of the Lord, by what right is this done? Who is he really that he merits such treatment? Julian's vision is that at the root of the human soul, symbolized in the parable by the servant, Christ dwells. What is actually at the bottom of our hearts? It is the indwelling Lord:

> I saw the soul as wide as it were an endless citadel, and also as it were a blessed kingdom . . . In the midst of that city sits our Lord Jesus, true God and true man . . . He sits erect there in the soul, in peace and in rest, and he rules and guards heaven and earth and everything that is.[36]

In a very real sense for Julian the servant is actually the Son. And although Julian has taken her time to reach this point after her initial vision of the bleeding crucifix at the beginning of the book, it is this which is her legacy theologically speaking. Human beings are constantly indwelt by the Son who sits in

the soul 'in peace and at rest', and the Father encloses all things
in his love as a mother encloses her children in her arms. Julian's
own struggle was to wake up to this truth, and as we have read
through her text we have seen how she has struggled to come
to terms with this, so difficult and alien to the current teaching of the Church did it seem. But her writing is also a call to
us to awake to the truth about our status before God and to
rejoice that this is the case. Sadly this is a legacy which has been
ignored or lost in the development of the Church, put aside by
the Protestant Reformation and then even more firmly locked
away by the Enlightenment emphasis on rationality as supreme.
Maybe Julian's vision is a reaction to the difficulties of the Church
of her day, for it is not surprising that she or anyone else would
prefer Christ reigning within the soul to Henry Despenser
reigning over the Church supposedly as Christ's representative,
and it was not just Julian who said so. Many Lollards went to
their deaths for saying as much. But the important point is that
it is only now, as the influence of the modern mindset wanes,
as the stranglehold of rationality is loosened and weakens, that
we can see the importance of Julian's vision and return to it
and embrace its legacy wholeheartedly.

What then can we say of Julian? We have seen already how
she represents the very English flowering of medieval women's
vernacular talk about God. We have recognized already that
this vision has been eclipsed by the 'masculine' rise of the
Reformation and the Enlightenment where 'reason' is primary.
Julian differs from her other womanly colleagues in being far
more theological and less dependent upon her emotional side
– 'in my understondying' is a common phrase. We have also
seen how the short text is hardly more than a statement of what
happened to Julian in 1373. The long text, written some fifteen
or twenty years later, shows that meditation on her original vision
leads Julian to a radical view of a God without wrath who is our
Mother. The very centrality of the parable of the Lord and the
servant in the long text should make it clear to contemporary

readers that Julian's principal concern is not with something called spirituality, not with the experience of proximity to God but with the problems of reconciling a vision of God's indwelling love with the traditions of the Church and the condition of the nation. Rebellion of the human soul is replaced by zeal. Her whole purpose is to resolve a struggle to reconcile the existence of sin and teaching of the Church about judgement, with her vision of the lack of wrath in God and an intrinsic lack of rebellion in humanity. That is precisely why the parable of the Lord and the servant is central in any attempt to understand Julian and why an emphasis on her theology of Christ as our 'Mother' is only incidentally, although very surely, a support for a more inclusive theology of gender in God and the Church. It is more importantly a consequence of a different way of seeing how God is towards us and of how she behaves towards humanity. To reduce the importance of Julian to being no more than a medieval support for contemporary concerns is to reduce her meaning absolutely.

Julian's primary legacy, therefore, is an enormously powerful understanding of the participation of the human person in God in which all the ills of the world are redeemed by love. As over against prevailing medieval nominalist philosophy – itself the precursor of the Enlightenment, as a number of contemporary theologians have recently shown[37] – in which things are each radically separate and individual, Julian argues that this world is not a separate reality, separate from the love of God, but is constantly interpenetrated by that love. There is no such thing as 'pure nature'. Thus this world is not entirely 'free' as modern liberal theology would posit. But this also means that the world is not so 'free' from God that it can be defined and ruled by secular or ecclesiastical powers. Behind everything, behind all appearances of independence, it is still God's. He still has his hands upon it without fail, 'How should anything be amiss?' Thus Julian calls for her readers, her 'even Christen', to wake up and to realize that they actually occupy a new or

different 'body' which is united with Christ in his 'Godly will'. This new body is the place where redemption is known and is wide and fair enough for all humanity. This was a totally different vision to the style of church life so earnestly defended by Henry Despenser, bishop of Norwich, where the enclosed and independent citadel of 'Christendom' was defended by force and kept in order by obedience.

We do not know when Julian died. There is some evidence that she was still alive in 1416. Whenever she died she was probably unaware of the beginnings of the Italian Renaissance at the beginning of the fifteenth century. But I would surmise that had she still been alive and had she been able to see the painting of the *Madonna della Misericordia* in the small town of Borgo san Sepulcro she would have recognized how it embodies her theology. This picture was painted by Piero della Francesca in 1442, only 26 or so years after the last known reference to Julian in England. Here is Mary holding out her cloak of mercy and enclosing within it all those who seek redemption, from a sinister hooded figure on one side to a young maiden with beautiful hair on the other. It was a commission from the Guild of Mercy which was devoted to the relief of the poor in that small town. Somehow Piero della Francesca understood what Julian was saying, how God 'Wrappith us and all beclosyth us'.

Nor is any of this simply a recipe for self-satisfaction. It has consequences for how we are in the world.

> Christians can have hope in disaster. Julian's words 'all shall be well' are not a counsel of inaction. Rather, the belief that every event is enfolded in the being and action of God can liberate Christians from the tedious need to safeguard their lives, thus opening them to the risk of imitating Christ's compassion. In fact, I would dare say that only those who open themselves in such a way can truthfully speak the words, 'all shall be well'.[38]

4

Thomas Traherne and the reinvention of the world

On 8 May 1660 the English Parliament proclaimed that Charles, eldest son of Charles I, who had been in exile from 1642, had been the lawful king of England since the execution of his father in January 1649. This effectively ended 11 years of Puritan rule in England and on 23 May Charles returned from exile in Holland and entered London on his birthday, 29 May. To celebrate 'his Majesty's return to his Parliament', 29 May was made a public holiday, popularly known as 'Oak Apple Day', and Charles was crowned king in Westminster Abbey on 23 April 1661. Not only was the king restored to his parliament but the Church of England was re-established and the bishops once again took up their sees and their places in the House of Lords. Puritan ministers were removed from the parishes they occupied unless they accepted episcopal ordination and gave their assent to a new Act of Uniformity which was passed in 1662. The Book of Common Prayer became the official and permanent legal version of public prayer authorized by both Parliament and the Church for use in churches across the land. About one-fifth of the English clergy refused to submit and were cast out of the Church as nonconformists. These events were the signal for a new spirit of life and energy which began to flow openly though the land.

A few months after the restoration of the monarchy a 'Royal Society' was founded which was dedicated to establishing the truth of scientific matters through observation and experiment rather than from deductive logic and the citation of ancient authorities. Within a very short time this society was given the explicit support of the monarchy and a royal charter. Its establishment marked a significant shift of emphasis in intellectual thinking in the country and was instrumental in turning people's eyes towards new horizons and the achievements of the age of reason which was about to unravel itself across Europe.

The past years of Puritan rule had not, however, all been anti-intellectual. In Cambridge a group of philosophers had been at work for some time enlarging their philosophical and theological horizons. Many of them were fellows of Emmanuel College, and their interests straddled the newly established church and the newly established Royal Society. They were theologians as well as philosophers. Like the members of the Royal Society they supported the centrality of reason and sought an alternative philosophy to the prevailing academic Aristotelianism. They knew of the work of Descartes in France and some of them had been in correspondence with him. His *Discours de la Methode* had appeared anonymously in 1637. While they valued the role of human reason they also defended the existence of God and the immortality of the soul. They drew inspiration from Plato and the philosophers of the Italian Renaissance and asserted that the spirit or an immanent divine soul was the fundamental causal principal in the operations of nature. They have since become known as the Cambridge Platonists because of the important place that Plato played in their thinking, and the group included such figures as Henry More and Ralph Cudworth. They are evidence of the intellectual and theological debates which were alive at this time and also of the intense interest that there was in the created order and the place of humankind in that order.

So already we can see that in the latter half of the seventeenth century England was a melting-pot of ideas and influences, many from abroad. It was not simply a question of the defeat of Puritanism and its replacement by the established church and monarch. Nor was it a time of simply replacing an outmoded deductive logic with the new inductive method of the new science. Douglas Chambers in his thought-provoking study of the period[1] shows that in many ways people at this time both embraced and rejected the changes which were afoot, and many, especially Swift and Milton, saw in the 'reinvention of the world' that was happening around them something which gave them a profound unease. But nonetheless this was undoubtedly a time of new thinking about creation and the place of humanity within that creation; it was a time of resurgence of interest in Renaissance humanism; a time of fierce debate about the place of reason and experiment in science and of the role of the spirit in the natural world. Churchmen and theologians took up again an interest in the early fathers of the Church. Thomas Ken, who became Bishop of Bath and Wells in 1684, was an ardent student of the early church fathers and his library contained a number of volumes of their works. England was being opened up to a world of ideas and influences from which, to a certain degree, it had been excluded during the Commonwealth period. Puritanism had imposed its own world view upon both church and state and upon the minds and hearts of men and women, while beneath it and beyond it new ways of seeing were being born.

In the midst of all this 'reinvention' and soon after the restoration of Charles II as king of England, a clergyman who was the vicar of a country parish not far from Hereford wrote a poem celebrating the restoration of church and state. The poem was called 'Bells', for the ringing of bells had been banned under the Commonwealth and this particular clergyman was obviously delighted that bells could once more ring out across the countryside and call people to worship in a re-established church. His name was Thomas Traherne and he was the vicar of the parish of Credenhill. He wrote,

Hark! Hark my soul! The bells do ring,
And with a louder voice
Call many families to sing
His public praises and rejoice:

But in some ways it was surprising that this particular clergyman should write a poem of this sort. He had been brought
up in Hereford during the Civil War and had gone to Oxford
University as a Puritan where he had been a member of
Brasenose College under a renowned Puritan principal. On his
return he had been appointed to the parish of Credenhill in
1657 by the Commissioners for the Approbation of Public
Preachers and his appointment had received the support of a
number of well-known Puritan divines in the county. However,
in 1660, well before he was legally required to do so, he sought
episcopal ordination, and he conformed to the requirements of
the Act of Uniformity in 1662.

It might be thought that Traherne was trimming his sails
to the prevailing wind, as indeed a number of people did at
this time, including Traherne's friend Joanna Hopton who
had become a Catholic at the beginning of the Commonwealth
and then an Anglican at the end of it. But the evidence
from Traherne's writings is that he warmly supported the re-
establishment of the monarchy and the Church. He had clearly
become convinced of the rightfulness of the new order and spent
a lot of his time in its defence. Among the recently discovered
manuscripts of Traherne in Lambeth Palace Library there is one
entitled *A Sober View of Dr Twisses his Considerations*, in which
he proposes a solution to the controversy over the doctrine
of election, a longstanding controversy between Puritans and
others as to whether God predestined some to damnation and
whether or not humanity's free will had a role in the work of
salvation. Traherne not only shows himself to be very alive to
this debate, such that he writes a long treatise quoting many
of the leading contenders on all sides, but also shows that his
aim is to settle the mind of the Church. He says,

I will think myself happy if I . . . shall (in) any way be beneficial to the Church of God, either in promoting her public
peace or in satisfying her private doubtings.[2]

Meanwhile another Traherne manuscript, which has been given
the title *The Church's Year Book*,[3] contains meditations and
prayers for the liturgical period of the Church from Easter to
All Saints Day. This is plainly a book to accompany the observ-
ance of the Book of Common Prayer and draws from the
writings of other Anglicans, including Lancelot Andrewes,
Jeremy Taylor and George Herbert. Not long after this Bishop
Thomas Ken would do the same with an even wider source
of liturgical inspiration in his small handbook of devotion
which remains in his manuscript hand and unpublished in his
cathedral library at Wells. In his remarks upon the Traherne
text A. M. Allchin says,

> we can observe him both as a typical spokesman for the Church
> of England in his day, and also as one who has a particular
> concern to link the worship of the church with the hallowing
> of the world of nature. . . . we see his wholehearted belief in the
> unity of the church and the nation, and in the conjunction of
> the sacred and the secular. For him, as for Hooker, church and
> kingdom are two sides of the same reality. After the experiences
> of the Commonwealth, people had to choose between the idea
> of the 'gathered church' on the one side, and the idea of the
> national church on the other. There can be no question where
> Traherne stands on this issue.[4]

So at one level Traherne is a clergyman who has, perhaps
by experience as well as by conviction, been persuaded of the
need for a national church and is concerned in his writings
to further that end in an eirenic and rational manner. As the
editor of the newly discovered manuscripts of Traherne says in
his introduction,

> At the Restoration Traherne was ready to take his place as a
> public minister, conscientiously conforming with full agreement

to the Thirty-Nine Articles, hoping to make his contribution to the peaceful establishment of a unified church.[5]

All of this lifts Traherne out of the niche that he has occupied in the minds of many for some years, namely as a devotional writer who has little concern for the affairs of this world and is perhaps naively concerned with the recovery of innocence and an unimaginable divine glory. A superficial 'spiritual' reading of Traherne's *Centuries of Meditations* – for so long almost the only text by which Traherne has been widely known – has to some extent been complicit in this interpretation. But as we shall see, a more careful look at the *Centuries* and a reading of the new manuscripts which grace his name will show that Traherne is very much a man of his time, making a real contribution to the theological and intellectual life of his day, indeed an important and intelligent theologian who has a great deal to say about the human condition and its relationship not just to the creation but also to God. Denise Inge, who has recently edited a selection of Traherne's texts, a selection which includes extracts from the newly discovered manuscripts, makes an important observation in her introduction when she says,

> And as modern scholarship applies itself to these texts, a hitherto 'alienated' Traherne is being replaced by a more integrated Traherne. Traherne the naïve woodland warbler sequestered away in his country parish becomes Traherne the public priest and private chaplain, a scholar and a theologian more concerned with the theological and political struggles of his day than we had ever imagined.[6]

But it is a common mistake of those concerned with 'spirituality' to wrench those they love to quote from their context. We have already seen how this has affected the interpretations of Meister Eckhart and Julian of Norwich and how a contextual look at their work can shed new light on how they related to their own day as well as re-vivify what they say for our own.

Such a contextual understanding enables those of us who live in the days of the demise of modernism and the rise of the frighteningly postmodern to see how such writers possess a much more profound significance than a simple 'spiritual' interpretation allows and perhaps enable us to live in these empty days with greater assurance and wakefulness to the transcendent. Traherne is a particularly good example of how this can occur because of his understanding of the natural world.

We know the outline of his life. He was born in Hereford in 1636, the son of a shoemaker who was able to employ a number of assistants. His parents died when he was young and the Civil War broke out when he was only six years old. Hereford was a garrison town and changed hands three times during the course of the war. As we have seen, Traherne was educated at Brasenose College in Oxford and returned to Hereford to take up the position of minister to the parish of Credenhill, some four or five miles to the north-west of the city. After his episcopal ordination in 1660 he remained the parish priest there until his death, but in 1669 he was also appointed Chaplain to Sir Orlando Bridgeman, Keeper of the Seal, and died at Bridgeman's house in Teddington in 1674 at the young age of 38. He does not seem to have neglected his parish in any way, for in 1673 his church-warden is noted as saying, 'Our minister is continually resident amongst us.' He was said to be 'a good and godly man, well learned . . . a good liver' who 'visited the poor and instructed the youth'. In 1671 and 1672 he is recorded as acting for the Dean of Hereford's Consistory Court, and was described by one of the canons of the cathedral as 'one of the most pious and ingenious men' he had known.[7] All of which confirms what we have already deduced, that Thomas Traherne was a loyal and devout minister of the Church of England who was active, intelligent, well read and well connected. His chaplaincy to the Keeper of the Great Seal and his household would have afforded him the opportunity to keep in touch with the intellectual and theological developments of the day.

He has left us a body of work which has grown enormously as new manuscripts have come to light over the last hundred years. He wrote poetry and prose, meditative works as well as expositions of the nature of ethics, treatises on the controversies of the day and devotional works to assist those who followed the Book of Common Prayer. For many years the principal work by which he was known was the *Centuries of Meditations*, first brought to light and published by Bertram Dobell in 1903. It is this work which can give the impression of a solitary who had turned his face from the world and secluded himself in the countryside, but which is deceptive in this regard, for on closer examination it is the entry point into a way of understanding that is clearly the result of considerable reflection on the whole Christian spiritual tradition in the context of the developments in natural science which were occurring in Traherne's day.

The genesis of the *Centuries* can be found in the third sequence of meditations, where Traherne reflects upon his experiences as a youth and his search for what he calls 'felicity'. The sequence begins with the glimpses of glory and innocence with which a child is born, but moves to show how these glimpses are spoiled.

> The first light which shined in my infancy in its primitive and innocent clarity was totally eclipsed: insomuch that I was fain to learn all again. If you ask me how it was eclipsed? Truly by the customs and manners of men, which like contrary winds blew it out: by an innumerable company of other objects, rude, vulgar and worthless things, that like so many loads of earth and dung did overwhelm and bury it. All men's thoughts and words were about other matters. They all prized new things which I did not dream of. . . . And finding no one syllable in any man's mouth of those things, by degrees they vanished . . . and at last all the celestial, great and stable treasures to which I was born, as wholly forgotten, as if they had never been.[8]

He reflects upon his time at university and sees there a further glimpse of things he had never dreamed existed, 'glorious secrets and glorious persons past imagination'. But nothing is taught, he complains, about felicity, and no thought was given to the purpose of learning. He moves through the subjects of his education drawing out the essential purpose which, he says, so many easily miss and so acquire learning as a possession rather than as a gift.

> Many men study the same things which have not the taste of, nor delight in them . . . He that studies polity, men and manners, merely that he may know how to behave himself, and get honor in this world, has not that delight in his studies as he that contemplates these things that he might see the ways of God among them . . . he is nothing if he knows them merely for talk or idle speculation, or transient and external use.[9]

But the sequence goes on to record the turning-point in Traherne's life when he returns to the countryside and resolves to live in search of felicity all of his days.

> When I came into the country, and being seated among silent trees, had all my time in my own hands, I resolved to spend it all, whatever it cost me in search of happiness.[10]

There is no artificial distinction in Traherne between town living and country living, as if one is superficial and leads to the loss of innocence and the other automatically grants felicity. This distinction is a modern invention. He is rather concerned to show how life is gift just as the creation is gift and that we are part of that gift and can live within it as part of it. This is the purpose of the first sequence of meditations. He writes,

> You never enjoy the world aright till the sea itself floweth in your veins, till you are clothed with the heavens and crowned with the stars, and perceive yourself to be the sole heir of the whole world, and more than so because men are in it who are

every one sole heirs as well as you. Till you can sing and rejoice and delight in God as misers do in gold and kings in sceptres you never enjoy the world.[11]

Such passages are reflected in Traherne's poetry, especially in the poem 'Wonder' where he speaks of arriving in this world as an angel:

How like an Angel came I down!
How bright are all things here!
When first among his works I did appear
O how their glory did me crown!
The world resembled his eternity,
In which my soul did walk;
And everything that I did see
Did with me talk.

And this is picked up again at the beginning of the third Century where, in a justly celebrated passage, he says,

The corn was orient and immortal wheat, which never should be reaped nor was ever sown. I thought it had stood from ever-lasting to everlasting. The dust and stones of the street were as precious as gold. The gates were at first the end of the world; the green trees when I saw them first through one of the gates transported and ravished me; ... their sweetness and unusual beauty made my heart to leap, and almost mad with ecstasy they were such strange and wonderful things. The men! O what venerable and reverend creatures did the aged seem! Immortal cherubims! And young men glittering and sparkling angels, and maids strange seraphic pieces of life and beauty! Boys and girls tumbling in the street and playing were moving jewels. I knew not that they were born or should die. But all things abided eternally as they were in their proper places. Eternity was manifest in the light of day, and something infinite behind everything appeared, which talked with my expectation and moved my desire. The city seemed to stand in Eden, or to be built in heaven.[12]

One might be tempted, on reading these extracts, to think that there was something naive and simplistic about Traherne. Indeed many have moved, somewhat prematurely, to this conclusion. Is he aware of the difficulties that beset human beings? What does he know of tragedy and sin? Such a critique is not only premature, it is also unseeing, for what Traherne is doing is searching for meaning in this troubled existence – and his upbringing and early years in Hereford would have made him sufficiently aware of the troubles that beset England at this time – and finding theological meaning within and beyond these troubles. Indeed it is precisely because he is so aware of the troubles that beset human beings that he writes as he does. For instance it is precisely because he is aware of the difficulties that a Puritan view of human nature causes that he writes as he does about childhood and innocence. Douglas Chambers, writing about the understanding of childhood in the literature of this period,[13] shows that there is in some writers of the period a shift from a negative to a positive view of childhood. Henry Vaughan and Thomas Traherne are representative of this shift and stand over against the ideas of the Puritan John Bunyan and, somewhat later, the hymn writer Isaac Watts in this regard. Henry Vaughan had written,

> Happy those early days! When I
> Shined in my angel-infancy![14]

Traherne echoes these sentiments some years later. In 1693 the philosopher John Locke wrote *Some Thoughts Concerning Education* and said that the child's mind was an empty space – *tabula rasa* – and we should therefore be careful what we placed in that space. But whereas Locke excluded fantasy and fairy tales as possibly harmful, Traherne allows the place of imagination and intuitive knowledge as part of the education of a child. But what both Locke and Traherne are saying is that later wisdom and maturity will grow from an education based upon a positive rather than a negative understanding of early childhood. Traherne writes,

> To Infancy, O Lord, again I come,
> That I my Manhood may improve;
> My early tutor is the womb;
> I still my cradle love;
> 'Tis strange that I should wisest be,
> When least I could an error see.[15]

So Traherne's emphasis upon the innocency of childhood is not a vague romantic naivety but a carefully judged view, in the context of seventeenth-century debates about the nature of education, of the way in which the view people have of the nature of a child affects the child's behaviour in later life. For him and others mature human behaviour comes from an education which affirms the positive in human nature. Goodness springs from a belief in goodness in the child.

But even to stop there would not be enough. There is more to the *Centuries* than a view about how best to understand and educate children. As one reads through these meditations one is taken into a different way of seeing things, a different set of perspectives, not only about the countryside or about the people who live there, but about how to understand things in general. Traherne's move to the countryside and his move from Puritanism to Anglicanism were the triggers for a different way of seeing everything. In this way of seeing things one particular insight is basic, namely that everything communicates with, and in a real sense is part of, everything else. The result is a life of joy. Traherne lives with open eyes all of the time, rejoicing in what he finds and believing that it is all one and all united and all a gift. He welcomes the world. It is often pointed out that Traherne took great interest in the scientific discoveries of his day and responded to the developments of his time not by withdrawing into a defensiveness about God's agency in creation, a defensiveness which has characterized a great deal of Christian thinking since Darwin, but by enlarging his theology and embracing the new discoveries and complementing them with his studies of the scriptures and the major writers of the Christian spiritual tradition. He did not feel that he had to build up faith as a bulwark against change in order to ensure that what was of value or true survived in this reinvented world. On the contrary he allowed this reinvention to enlarge his own faith and met the new with an even larger vision. As one contemporary theologian has written, perceptively,

> he meets the new enlarged horizons with an even larger one – a fresh conception of the infinity of God in interaction with creation, in which the new scientific discoveries play a part. He responds to confidence in human thought and pride in human freedom not by detracting from humanity but by stretching his thinking in order to do justice to God as well as to all that is known about the world, and by revelling in the risk God takes in allowing the completion of creation to rely on human freedom. He is impatient with 'divines and schoolmen' who have interpreted the image of God in humanity far too constrictedly, leaving out the most wonderful aspects of God.[16]

So Traherne's reflections upon the countryside and upon the innocency of childhood are but a gateway into a new set of perspectives about the way in which looking at things with open eyes can enlarge our understanding of God so that we are transformed by joy into God's image. In his work *Select Meditations*, Traherne takes the 'divines and schoolmen' to task for not having seen this, or at least for having spoken of it superficially. Traherne says that God,

> Being infinite in bounty, and willing to make his image, he made a creature like him to behold all ages and to love the goodness of every being in all eternity, and of every excellence in every being. That by seeing, it might receive, and enjoy by loving, all the things in heaven and earth.[17]

Indeed God made the world for our enjoyment, and its very superabundance, its *excess* as the postmoderns would call it, is there for us to share in and be caught into.

> To see His wisdom, goodness and power employed in creating all worlds for our enjoyment, and infinitely magnified in beautifying them for us, and governing them satisfies our self-love; but with all it so obligeth us that in love to Him, which it createth in us, maketh us more to delight in those attributes as they are His, than as they are our own. . . . But now there is an infinite union between Him and us, He being infinitely delightful to us, and we to Him.[18]

This intensity of joy exists not just between God and his creation and between God and us but also between us and others. Moreover as we enjoy each other and ourselves so we are transformed and redeemed.

But there are other themes in the *Centuries* which require comment. One of them is the theme of 'wanting' which occurs regularly in these meditations. Traherne has already implied, as we will have gathered from the extracts we have quoted, that God wants and even needs the reciprocal love of human beings. It is almost as if God only exists when the love and delight which he pours out upon and through his creation is returned to him. He comments that this is a strange thing.

> This is very strange that God should want. For in him is the fullness of all Blessedness. He overfloweth eternally. His wants are as glorious as infinite: perfective needs that are in his nature, and ever Blessed because always satisfied. He is from all eternity full of want . . . Want is the fountain of his fullness. Want in God is treasure to us. For had there been no need He would not have created the world, nor made us, nor manifested his wisdom . . . But he wanted Angels and Men, Images, Companions: and these he had from all eternity.[19]

But then he goes on to say that if God wants then we must want in return.

You must want like a god that you may be satisfied like God. Were you not made in his image? . . . Be present with your want of a Deity, and you shall be present with the Deity. You shall adore and admire him, enjoy and prize him; believe in him and delight in him, see him to be the fountain of all your joys and the head of all your treasures.[20]

This theme is picked up again in the poem 'Desire', where Traherne says,

For giving me desire,
An eager thirst, a burning ardent fire,
A virgin, infant flame,
A love with which into the world I came,
An inward, hidden heavenly love
Which in my soul did work and move
And ever, ever me inflame
With restless longing, heavenly avarice
That never could be satisfied,
That did incessantly a paradise
Unknown suggest, and something undescried
Discern, and bear me to it; be
Thy name forever praised by me.

These words, especially the words, 'That did incessantly a paradise unknown suggest, and something undescried discern, and bear me to it' should give us some clue as to what Traherne is talking about. Already we have seen how the group of philosophers known as the Cambridge Platonists believed that the spirit or the divine soul was immanent throughout the universe, and Traherne's words here are certainly not far from that sentiment, and we know that Traherne had read and was much influenced by the Cambridge group, but there is even more to it than that. For the Christian spiritual tradition had for a long time understood that what filled the universe was a spirit of yearning or longing, a yearning or longing which came from God and which returned to God, a spirit or force which the earliest fathers knew as

Eros. The sixth-century writer now known as Pseudo-Denys wrote,

> It must be said that the very cause of the universe is the beautiful, good superabundance of his benign yearning (eros) for all is carried outside of himself in the loving care he has for everything.[21]

Seeing God as the source of Eros as well as the point of return for Eros permeates Christian spiritual writing right through until the Reformation. Much of the biblical inspiration for this came from the Song of Songs, which was the scriptural text which received the greatest amount of comment and commentary until its influence was eclipsed during the Reformation. The book has never really recovered its status until recent years when feminist scholars in particular have resurrected its importance. As is well known, the Song of Songs was of crucial importance for St Bernard and the Cistercian movement, and John of the Cross was so inspired by its sense of longing for God in the dark that much of his poetry as well as his prose was modelled upon it. He asked for it to be read to him as he lay dying in 1591. In his great study of the use of the Song of Songs by medieval writers, Professor Denys Turner says,

> we are forced to conclude that it was not in spite of the Song's eroticism but because of it, that Gregory, Bernard, Alan, and Denys, and a hundred other mediaeval commentators, warmed to this text. To the authors of this unbroken thousand years of commentarial tradition, the natural, spontaneous, but also reflectively apt, human model for divine love is love in its erotic expression.[22]

It is this tradition that Traherne picks up when he speaks of 'Desire' and of 'wanting' in God. He, more than any other English post-Reformation writer, and because of his reading of the early Fathers and the Cambridge Platonists, keeps this tradition alive for the Church. Others do not neglect it, and indeed Henry

Vaughan explicitly uses imagery from the Song of Songs in his great poem 'The Night', where he writes of

> God's silent, searching flight:
> When my Lord's hand is filled with dew, and all
> His locks are wet with the clear drops of night;

which is a direct quotation from chapter 5 of the Song of Songs. But it is Traherne who seizes upon the essence of this tradition and expounds it in his own way throughout the text of the *Centuries*.

But even that is not sufficient. For Traherne God is the source of infinite attraction for humanity. Through God's desire for them men and women are drawn to God. The point at which this divine attraction is exercised and the gateway through which men and women have to pass into God is, of course, the life and death of Jesus. In particular it is the cross of Christ which forms the fulcrum or sacrament for this divine attraction. Traherne writes,

> The Cross is the abyss of wonders, the centre of desires, the school of virtues, the house of wisdom, the throne of love, the theatre of joys, and the place of sorrows; It is the root of happiness, and the gate of heaven.[23]

He continues,

> The cross of Christ is the Jacob's ladder by which we ascend into the highest heavens.[24]

So for Traherne our 'wanting' returns to God and the cross is the point of 'return' to God. Through this point of divine attraction we are drawn back into the life of God and away from 'this world'. So the cross is central to Traherne's thinking, in spite of so much comment since the publication of the *Centuries* that his theology of the cross was deficient. It manifestly is central to his thought, but not in the way that the cross has often been understood by the post-Reformation Church.

But Traherne is attracting more and more attention, and there has been a great deal of interest expressed in the manuscripts discovered in Lambeth Palace Library in 1997. One of the treatises discovered there is entitled *The Kingdom of God* and, of all of Traherne's works, it is this which shows how cognizant he was of the new scientific discoveries of the age. It is also in this work that he not only embraces such discoveries but develops a view of God which embraces and encompasses them. His God is not privatized in reaction to these discoveries. He speaks of how God pours himself out in the work of creation, comparing creation to a mother's milk which cannot remain in her breasts but has to be expressed,

> His wisdom easily and sweetly passeth through all from end to end. The streams by which it overflows are as sweet unto it as a nurse's milk is to her in its effusions, which is if withheld of no delight.[25]

He goes on to say that God goes out of himself into his creation.

> He that is out of himself and in himself together is greater than he that is shut up and confined, abiding in himself alone. God is infinite in himself and in his kingdom too. He is wholly out of himself, as well as wholly in himself. I may say he poured out himself when he proceeded to his work, and that God himself is the life and beauty of the same, who is as great in the Holy Spirit as in the first person of his eternal essence; as great in his kingdom, as in himself; since his Holy Spirit entirely proceedeth from him and really dwelleth in all the creatures.[26]

Such passages as these link Traherne inextricably with the earlier spiritual tradition of the Church. The outpouring of God himself in his creation, his exiting of himself, is one of the great themes of this tradition and is found especially in Meister Eckhart. Eckhart speaks of the way in which God 'boils over' in his creation. For Eckhart the Trinity is a sort of boiling pot in which God constantly gives birth to himself but then, in creation, this intensity of mutual self-giving boils over and pours itself forth (*ebulliat*). But this way of looking at things also links Traherne to the scientific world of the twenty-first century where it is becoming increasingly clear that the creation is not static nor the product of a creator who has remained static in himself. For present-day scientists creation is not static and as it was at the beginning, but a constant effusion, a continual creation and recreation of itself which, effectively, 'boils' with life. Even a moderately conservative scientist and theologian such as John Polkinghorne can say,

> I certainly believe that the distant God of classical theism, existing in isolated transcendence, is a concept in need of correction by a recovered recognition of the immanent presence of the creator to the creation.[27]

Although it is a puzzle as to where Polkinghorne gets this 'classical' doctrine, for the earlier theologians knew of the way in which God was both in himself and out of himself at the same time, it is clear is that here is a point of convergence between modern scientific understanding and the Christian tradition as represented not just by Traherne but by so many others. What is remarkable is that Traherne has preserved this tradition within the English church. Donald Allchin says,

> Thomas Traherne stands at a crucial moment in the development of the Anglican tradition, when the old world of the patristic and medieval synthesis was in touch with the first beginnings of the scientific movement represented by the Royal Society.[28]

It is because Traherne stands at this point and relishes the fact that he does so and makes his presence at such a point work for himself that he is of such significance for those of us who have not yet succeeded in relating the two worlds with either the panache or the style that he brought to this work.

But while that should be significant enough, there is still more to say. On reading Traherne what overwhelms the reader is the enormous sense of thankfulness and joy which pervades his work. He reintroduces us to the idea of happiness, what he calls 'felicity'. Indeed he urges happiness upon us as that which God wills for us and for all of his creation. This takes us somewhat by surprise because we are used to being urged to find or achieve salvation. What we find difficult is the view that God holds out happiness, 'felicity', to us as gift if only we would open our eyes and see. Traherne's view is that we have our eyes far too focused upon our own situation and have become embroiled in human possessions and human achievements to such an extent that we cannot see what is in fact the case. For Traherne it is contact with nature which has opened his eyes to this truth, but to remain at that point and to classify Traherne as a sort of nature mystic, as some have done, is totally inadequate. His contact with nature releases him into a totally different theological world where incorporation into the life of God is offered to all and he goes on to expound this incorporation in the theological terms developed by an earlier generation of Christian thinkers. Moreover, he not only speaks to a frenzied age such as ours of the importance of happiness but he is also a challenge to the contemporary Church which is preoccupied with change, evangelism and other forms of activism which simply mirror rather than challenge the spirit of the age. But most importantly it is his insistence that thankfulness and joy are the gift of God and bring those who discover and exercise them into relationship with the life of God that brings him into contact with the longstanding earlier traditions of Christian understanding.

It is this which another contemporary theologian, Mark McIntosh, has seen so clearly in Traherne. McIntosh points out that from the beginning the path to salvation had always been seen by Christian thinkers as a path which led out of knowing and possessing things for themselves into knowing and possessing things as they are in themselves and then moving from there into an act of thanksgiving for all things, including the self, as gift, gift which is the gift of God. This leads the soul out of prison into the light of God. He quotes Augustine who says that the life of faith aims at

> obtaining those inner and higher things that are not possessed privately but in common by all who love them, possessed in a chaste embrace without any limitations or envy.[29]

This, of course, is to possess things as gift. McIntosh shows how Traherne exemplifies this in so many ways and brings to Christian thinking a deep sense of participation in the mystery of God by enjoyment of, and thankfulness for, all that is. He comments,

> Perhaps it is a little hard for us to imagine quite what Traherne, along with Augustine, Maximus, Bonaventure, and Aquinas, has in mind with all this. We are so very used to thinking of things purely in their merely physical form. . . . Traherne was writing at the very dawn of this era in modern science, and in many ways he would rejoice that we have so far penetrated into the deeper level of gifts that God pours out to us in all the creatures. But I think Traherne would also remind us that humanity will never understand the world aright so long as we limit ourselves to a merely reductive reading of things.[30]

And McIntosh quotes Traherne's meditation (*Centuries*, 2.90) where he says that to offer God things back to him in praise is more precious than the original gifting of things by God to us. McIntosh goes on,

> By lifting up all things in the act of praise, the mind is able to translate them, so to speak, back into their native tongue, which is the language of pure giving and receiving. . . . Things are no longer things, but moments of relationship, events in the life of heaven begun on earth.[31]

All this, of course, places Traherne very firmly in the mystical tradition of the Church and in the tradition of affirmative mysticism at that. So from the historical moments surrounding

his life, the move from Puritanism to Anglicanism at the restoration of church and monarchy, from the move from Oxford
and the schools back to the countryside, from his debates
with Puritans and others over the education of children
and his reading of the Renaissance thinkers and the early
Fathers, Traherne moves into a long and illustrious tradition
of apophatic mystics. But what this survey of Traherne's
thought should show us is that mysticism is not, emphatically
not, a matter of escaping from the world in order to discover
God in the flight of the alone to the alone. Indeed it was precisely because Traherne involved himself in the discoveries of
the day that he grew into a mystical awareness. What he saw
entranced and dazzled him. He literally 'woke up' to reality.

Our study of the work of Meister Eckhart showed that the
negative mystical way which he followed was a form of breakdown of language in the face of the glory of God. The affirmative mystical way also faces the glory of God, but in the face of
such glory finds itself forced to use metaphor after metaphor
in order to talk about such glory adequately. While the negative mystic finds language inadequate, the affirmative mystic finds
a restricted language pattern inadequate. Modern students of
mysticism, who include Archbishop Rowan Williams as well
as academic figures such as Denys Turner and Grace Jantzen,
see the popular view of mysticism, based on the writings of
William James, as a mistake. In this popular view mysticism
is associated with particular Christian individuals and is a
form of spiritual or deeply personalized experiential faith. It
is the mystical experience of some people. Very often this can
be detached from common worship, sacraments, doctrine or
church organization and is said to be found in all religions and
is often regarded as the basis of all religion. Research into the
mystical texts by scholars like Rowan Williams, whose book on
Teresa of Ávila is of capital importance, or Grace Jantzen,
whose work on Julian has become standard, would maintain
that mysticism cannot be divorced from the ongoing life of the

Church. For them mysticism is better defined, perhaps, as the result of living the faith in great depth and with great discipline within the liturgical community of the Church. This has the effect of enabling the believer to see the glory of God in and through all things and to be blinded by his glory in what has been called either 'a ray of darkness' (John of the Cross) or 'a dazzling darkness' (Henry Vaughan). Seeing the glory of God in all things is the affirmative (or cataphatic) way, wheras to be blinded by glory is the negative (or apophatic) way.

Denys Turner remarks,

> What then of the 'cataphatic'? The cataphatic is, we might say, the verbose element in theology, it is the Christian mind deploying all the resources of language in the effort to express something about God, and in that striving to speak, theology uses as many voices as it can. It is the cataphatic in theology which causes its metaphor-ridden character, causes it to borrow vocabularies by analogy from many another discourse, whether of science, literature, art, sex, politics, the law, the economy, family life, warfare, play, teaching, physiology or whatever. . . . For in its cataphatic mode, theology is, we might say, a kind of verbal riot . . .[32]

If this is true then Traherne, with his verbal excess and his borrowings from the world of science of his day, cannot but be classified as a cataphatic or affirmative mystical writer. Traherne's writings bear comparison with so many other affirmative texts, from Julian through Bernard of Clairvaux to Edwin Muir in our own day. These accounts are usually deeply positive, or at least they result in a deeply positive awareness of creation and the self as part of the creation. In them even the self is beautiful. Moreover such accounts show that such awareness is 'given'. It just happens, usually after a long time in the Christian life. Such awareness is not self-generated; it seems to come from somewhere else. You cannot make these things happen or predict when they will happen. All of the accounts talk as if there is someone else, a greater force, who is 'hidden' behind the reality which we can all see, but to which that reality and the speaker belongs. This reality appears shot through with divine life. The accounts also show that the people who recount them then turn to live a more settled secure and faithful life. Cataphatic mystical accounts are, therefore, not 'private' and not 'personal' since everything is involved in them. They are not 'ecstatic' and they are essentially bound up with how the participants then behave. As so many writers aver, you cannot be a mystic and not behave in a serious moral way. There are different ways in which cataphatic awareness comes about. Sometimes the accounts are given by people who have given things up, either voluntarily or involuntarily. Brian Keenan's well-known mystical experience of the presence of an orange in solitary confinement in the Lebanon, recounted in his moving book, *An Evil Cradling*, is plainly a result of an involuntary *ascesis*, but it became meaningful and central to the rest of his life. The poet and writer Edwin Muir, who died in 1959, has left us one of the most beautifully expressed and searching accounts of an affirmative awareness in his poem, 'The Transfiguration', where he writes,

> So from the ground we felt that virtue branch
> Through all our veins till we were whole, our wrists
> As fresh and pure as water from a well,
> Our hands made new to handle holy things,
> The source of all our seeing rinsed and cleansed
> Till earth and light and water entering there
> Gave back to us the clear unfallen world.
> We would have thrown our clothes away for lightness,
> But that even they, though sour and travel stained,
> Seemed, like our flesh, made of immortal substance . . .[33]

Nor is such a vision restricted to prose or poetry or to a former age, for the work of the artists Samuel Palmer and Robin Tanner share his engagement with the transcendental nature of the English countryside. Meanwhile in the 1970s an American biologist, Annie Dillard spent a year in the Shenandoah Valley in Vermont and wrote an amazing account of her stay there, *Pilgrim at Tinker Creek.* She writes of the importance of 'seeing'. There are two ways of seeing, she says, the analytical and prying way of seeing is one, which is, she agrees, essential at one level.

> But there is another kind of seeing that involves a letting go. When I see this way I sway transfixed and emptied. . . . When I see this way I see truly. As Thoreau says, I return to my senses.[34]

Then she points out that this way of seeing is not self-generated and it links the seer with the whole spiritual tradition.

> But I can't go out and try to see this way. I'll fail, I'll go mad. All I can do is try to gag the commentator, to hush the noise of useless interior babble that keeps me from seeing just as surely as a newspaper dangled before my eyes. The effort is really a discipline requiring a lifetime of dedicated struggle; it marks the literature of saints and monks of every order East and West, under every rule and no rule, discalced and shod.[35]

And she concludes her diary,

> I think that the dying pray at the last not 'please', but 'thank you', as a guest thanks his host at the door. . . . Divinity is not playful. The universe was not made in jest but in solemn incomprehensible earnest. By a power that is unfathomably secret, and holy, and fleet. There is nothing to be done about it, but ignore it, or see. And then you walk fearlessly.[36]

Here we are in the presence of the same spirit which infused the work of Thomas Traherne some three hundred years previously.

But neither the language of Traherne nor the language of Annie Dillard is the language of conventional Christianity. Conventional Christianity has adopted, both prior to and since Traherne's day, an assumed 'basic' language, the language of so-called 'classical' theology. This language does not easily incorporate concepts such as 'felicity' or 'wanting' or 'desire' or the language of 'seeing' espoused by Annie Dillard. It is the language of redemption and atonement, of personal sin and the work of Jesus Christ. The difficulty with much of this 'classical' language is that it is not 'classical' at all but recent. In pre-modern times it hardly had the pre-eminence that it is now said to have had. It is a propositional style of language, concerned with 'truth' rather than 'seeing' and so owes more to the rise of Enlightenment thought and the place of reason and scientific proof than to mystery and metaphor. In many ways such language is an attempt to beat the modern world at its own game. Traherne's language, however, is pre-modern, or at least what is now called 'early modern', and so has much more affinity with the postmodern than perhaps has been realized. We have already seen how Traherne's talk of abundance is very similar to Eckhart's talk of *ebullitio* and the postmodern term 'excess'. But the similarities do not stop there. This is the perceptive thesis of another American theologian, A. Leigh DeNeef. DeNeef relates Traherne to the postmodern writers Heidegger, Lacan and Derrida. In particular he finds that Traherne's understanding of 'being' links him with the postmoderns because for Traherne 'being' is not closed. We are open to all things and only exist in relationship to them. Man is not, in Traherne's thinking, 'the end, the measure and recipient of all things, he has become instead the giver or bestower of all things'. DeNeef goes on to say,

> Traherne began his analysis of things with the simple wonder that they actually appear 'bright in their own light'. Now the circulation and the communication of that light brings man himself into unconcealment before God and God himself into caring presence with man. God like man needs and desires; and the things he most admires are the loving 'thanksgivings' of man. . . . Like Heidegger, Traherne is concerned with both the fullness and the authenticity of our responsiveness towards things – the manner in which we take pleasure in and treasure

them. Things therefore, are sites of relation between man and God, beings and Being as such.[37]

This very porosity of Traherne's thinking is of course something which has been taken up by postmodern thinkers who react against the centrality of Man and his positivist belief in things as objects and so his obsession with possession and control. DeNeef goes on to draw similar parallels between Traherne and Lacan's concept of 'desire' and his similarity to the idea of 'supplementarity' in the thinking of Derrida. DeNeef's argument is focused largely on what he calls 'the new historicism', and he is concerned to show that there is no basis for such historicism in either the Renaissance texts of Traherne or the postmodern texts he cites. The argument could equally well be used against the 'new classicism' in theological thinking, showing that there are greater continuities between the premodern and the postmodern and that the intervening attempts to link theology to a positivist or descriptive theology are mistaken.

Traherne's real legacy, however, is wakefulness and delight. He it is who urges us to move out of the prison of our self with a delight in all that is, a delight which enables us to share in the delight that God has in things, and so brings us back to the kingdom from which we have fallen through thoughtlessness.

5

'A balm for all wounds':
Paul Celan and Etty Hillesum

On 11 April 1987 the Italian writer Primo Levi threw himself down the stairwell of the house in which he had been born in Turin. Forty years previously Levi had spent the last years of the war in a concentration camp, Auschwitz-Birkenau, after his arrest working with partisans in northern Italy. As the war came to an end he and many others were abandoned by the departing Nazis and, after a long trail through Eastern Europe and Russia, he returned to Turin in 1945. His account of his incarceration in Auschwitz, *If This Is a Man*, had, by the time of his death, become recognized as the most important firsthand account of the Holocaust and essential reading for any concerned to understand something not just of the horror that was inflicted upon the Jews and others in those days, but also the dignity and humanity of one man's response to it.

Levi had some difficulty in finding a publisher for his memoir, perhaps because insufficient time had elapsed for the European psyche to absorb what had happened, but he was the first to recognize the importance of recording these events and of bringing them to the surface of human consciousness so that they could be recognized for what they were and so, hopefully, not repeated. Gradually, over the years since the end of the war, other records have emerged, sometimes in diary form, sometimes in poetry, sometimes as memoirs, and a great deal has been written about the events of and the reasons for the

Holocaust. Apart from the many accounts by historians and the even greater number of attempts to assess the meaning and significance of those days, there have also been a number of literary reactions. Among the best known of these is the novel by Thomas Keneally, *Schindler's Ark*, which became a celebrated film (*Schindler's List*) and is based upon actual events. But it is not often that these literary accounts deal with the impact of the horror of the Holocaust on our very capacity to speak meaningfully of God, or indeed to speak meaningfully any more. Nor does modern literature very often want to tackle the issues of evil and death. It is often, as Paul Celan himself recognized, no more than 'literature', scribblings which titillate but never come near to the real questions which have to be asked. But there are some theologians, Jewish and Christian, who have recognized that the Holocaust must make a significant difference to the way in which theology, talk about God, can be done. Rabbi Nicholas de Lange in his 1997 Cardinal Bea Memorial Lecture asked the question, 'Where was Jesus Christ at Auschwitz?', echoing for Christians the question posed by Elie Wiesel in his book *Night*, 'Where is God now?' as a child hung on a gibbet in Auschwitz but was unable to die because his weight was not sufficient. Some attempts have been made to come to terms with these questions. Others have been driven even further back, into a place where no words can be found, into silence. The German philosopher Theodor Adorno remarked, 'There is no poetry after Auschwitz,' while George Steiner has explored the whole crisis of the middle years of the twentieth century where the world of words shrinks in a 'retreat from the authority and range of verbal language'.[1] Even suicide might be described as a form of movement into silence in the face of horror, and it is noticeable that two of the Holocaust's most remarkable survivors and witnesses, Primo Levi and Paul Celan, both chose this way. The Holocaust requires words of explanation but also silence, silence in reverence for those who died but also silence before God; for at this point even God is silent and nothing can be said by him or to him. And so the links between those who attempt to say anything about the Holocaust and those who are forced into saying nothing about God in the mystical tradition become very close. Apophasis and silence in the face of God at this point are not so very far from each other.

The facts about the Holocaust are no longer in doubt. Somewhere near six million Jews were singled out and relieved of their legal rights, transported to labour camps, used and then destroyed along with countless others: misfits, gypsies and homosexuals. This genocide was in one sense no different from the genocides in Cambodia, Armenia, Bosnia and Rwanda in the twentieth century, although each has its own set of distinguishing features. What is in common is the desire of one powerful part of a society to rid itself of unwanted persons, and in this modern age such powerful groups find that they now have the means so to do. What characterized the Nazi Holocaust was an efficient transport system and the corrupt collaboration of industry hungry for labour. An efficient modern state had developed the means by which it could destroy those whom its philosophy had demonized. Meanwhile the Church had developed a post-Lutheran doctrine of the two kingdoms, a separation between the kingdom of God, entered by personal and private devotion, and the kingdom of this world, governed publicly by the state. Thus, as Karl Barth and then Dietrich Bonhoeffer discerned, the German church was paralysed, unable to criticize the Nazi state with any real theological energy and also unable to tackle the legacy within itself of a teaching of contempt towards the Jews. This teaching had soured the thought of the early Fathers of the Church and was deeply embedded in the work of Martin Luther himself who, in 1543, had urged his followers to

> set fire to their synagogues or schools and bury or cover with dirt whatever will not burn . . . this is to be done in honour of our Lord and of Christendom.[2]

It was, therefore, hardly surprising that on the night of 9 November 1938 this is exactly what happened when 119 synagogues, together with many Jewish shops and homes, were burned to the ground in Germany. The modern state ruled while the Church and private conscience looked within and away.

This at least should have demonstrated that the modern state is intrinsically unreliable. We now know that modernism does not guarantee moral goodness within society. It is not actually as good as the Enlightenment 'philosophes' believed it would be. We know now not only that the modern world brings war and conflict between nations and poverty to the developing world, but also that modern nations themselves contain enormous violence and deprivation. Modernism has produced a disenchanted world run for the benefit of the successful. Modernism and its belief in reason has led to little more than an emphasis on efficiency, which, in the absence of a search for a moral state as well as moral individuals, only allows or facilitates Holocaust whenever powerful factions wish to remove groups of people whom they have demonized.

The modern state relies upon what it believes to be sane and intelligent men for its ordering. But it was at the trial of one of these apparently sane and rational men, Adolf Eichmann, that the limitations of sanity became apparent, at least to one person who reflected upon Eichmann's demeanour at the trial. Eichmann had been one of those who ruled Auschwitz. He was eventually tracked down by the Israeli secret service and after a dramatic abduction put on trial in Jerusalem. Many remarked at the time on his aloof and undisturbed behaviour and on his defence that he did what he did under orders from others. In response to this Thomas Merton wrote,

> The sanity of Eichmann is disturbing . . . It is the sane ones, the well adapted ones, who can without qualms and without nausea aim the missiles and press the buttons that will initiate the great festival of destruction that they, the sane ones, have prepared . . . We can no longer assume that because a man is

'sane' he is therefore in his 'right mind.' The whole concept of sanity in a society where spiritual values have lost their meaning is in itself meaningless. A man can be sane in the limited sense that he is not impeded by his disordered emotions from acting in a cool, orderly manner, according to the needs and dictates of the social situation in which he finds himself. He can be perfectly 'adjusted.' God knows, perhaps such people can be perfectly adjusted even in hell itself . . . I am beginning to realise that 'sanity' is no longer a value or an end in itself. The 'sanity' of modern man is about as useful to him as the huge bulk and muscles of the dinosaur. If he were a little less sane, a little more doubtful, a little more aware of his absurdities and contradictions, perhaps there might be a possibility of his survival . . .[3]

This need for uncertainty of speech is what the Holocaust should bring out of those who would speak, especially those who would speak about God. In reality the Holocaust marks the end of modernism, or rather the failure of modernism, but reflection upon it should also bear fruit and bring about a shift in the way in which those who wish to speak about God find themselves able so to do. Whether or not this shift is called a shift from the modern to the postmodern is not so much the point. What should shift is the way in which we feel able to speak about God, otherwise the old theological imperatives, many of which have been indirectly implicated in both the rise and the fall of the modern state, will remain in place.

The importance of the Holocaust therefore is that it compels human beings to reflect upon the death-dealing capacity of the controlling ego-self. Nazism was in the grip, it is now agreed, of a conviction that it knew the truth about the place of the German nation, how it had been humiliated by others and ravaged by Jews and so now needed to control its own destiny. This conviction gave the soul of Germany into the hands of a death-dealing ego-self. 'Sanity' or rationality was no longer a guarantee of goodness or truth, however much the architects of the German state would claim to be, or even actually be, 'sane'. Sanity was overridden by something else. Furthermore, reflection on the Holocaust should lead us to try to recover the true nature of the self and to reconstitute this self in a new way, a way which does not deliver death to others who are regarded as unwanted for whatever reason. Post-modern thinkers show us that we have to move out of the old self and that who we are may be reconstituted as simply 'movement towards the other' or 'welcome to the other' including God.[4] Indeed, in this process some have recognized, as we shall see, that we have to take the risk that God himself will become silent and we, out of our silence, have to move towards him. So the Holocaust compels us to reflect upon the need for a different kind of speech. 'Chatter' or 'commentary', what Les Murray the Australian poet calls 'narrowspeak', or what Paul Celan called 'literature', is revealed – as superficial and classical theological language is revealed – as potentially oppressive. Apparently rational theological speech may even con-tribute to or collude with such horror. This means that language may be reconstituted, perhaps simply as 'word', or 'word out of silence'. Language can no longer be required to pass through so-called rational processes before it is recognized as valid.

Reflection upon the Holocaust as the end result of modernism could, indeed should, mean that humanity learns to accept and live by such a new way of being 'self' – 'self' simply defined as 'movement towards the other' or 'welcome to the other'. Such reflection should also enable us to develop a new way of 'speaking' about God. In other words theological talk is not talk which presumes to know what God is like or to describe God as if he were some sort of object we have encountered. It has to emerge slowly and with difficulty out of the depths of the soul recognizing that God is not the same as anything else, and that God cannot be described as if he (or she) has been directly seen. When that happens, but only when that happens, can we say that we are living theologically, that is 'before God'.[5]

We can look to two particular examples of how this can happen, two individuals who themselves lived through the Holocaust although they were both also effectively silenced by it. These are Paul Celan, a poet writing in German, and Etty Hillesum, a Dutch woman who wrote a diary. They were both Jews and both faced the extremes and forged new ways of speaking and seeing in response. It goes without saying that not only Jews but also and especially Christians might take their example to heart in the way they live and speak in the present age.

Paul Celan was born 1920 in Czernovitz, which is in present-day Romania. His birth name was Paul Antschel or Ancel. 'Celan' is an anagram of his name which he adopted when his poems first appeared in Romania. He was Jewish and started to study medicine in France, but after a while he returned home to study romance languages and literature. After the outbreak of war and the occupation of his country by the Nazis he and his family lived in the Jewish ghetto, but in 1942 his parents were deported, his father died and his mother was murdered. From that point Celan was confined to labour camps until the end of the war. After the war he went to Bucharest and then to Vienna, but eventually settled in Paris in 1948. He taught German literature at the Ecole Normale Supérieure and wrote and published poetry in German. He was awarded a number of prestigious literary prizes for his work, married and became well known as part of the European literary scene. Tragically, however, he committed suicide in 1970, since when his poetry has been anthologized and translated into English and is regularly the subject of commentary not only by poets but also by theologians.

Celan's poetry stands in the German lyric tradition, but as he develops his style it becomes more and more concentrated, more and more enclosed and to some extent dense and inscrutable. In fact he pushes language to its limits, such that a very close reading of the text is required where the signals put out by certain key words are subconsciously registered at a profound level by the reader. He was an admirer of the American poet Emily Dickinson, whose work is similarly concentrated and to some extent self-enclosed, and he translated her work into German and French. His dense minimalist language brought him some criticism, of course, but also recognition that there was a mystical edge to his work, as indeed there is to that of Emily Dickinson. In his prose work and in the speeches which accompanied his acceptance of the literary prizes he was awarded he spoke of his links with mystical thought, particularly that of the Jewish tradition. It is also clear that biblical imagery both from the New Testament and from the Hebrew scriptures helped to convey something of the intensity of his struggle to communicate. In his speech on the occasion of the award of the Georg Büchner Prize in 1960 Celan reminds his listeners that all poetry begins from certain dates, certain points which are a beginning for the poet. His 'date' is 20 January, which was the date of the Wansee Conference when the Final Solution to the Jewish question was agreed by the Nazis. He continues,

> But I think a hope of poems has always been to speak in just this way in the cause of the *strange* – no I can't use this word any more – in just this way to speak *in the cause of an Other* – who knows, perhaps in the cause of a wholly Other.[6]

And a little later he says,

> The poem wants to reach an Other, it needs this Other, it needs an Over-against. It seeks it out, speaks towards it. . . . What is addressed takes shape only in the space of this conversation, gathers around the I addressing and naming it. But what's addressed and is now become a Thou through naming, as it were, also brings along its otherness into this present.[7]

And it is not difficult to see this in his poetry where there is often a mysterious 'other' who is addressed. The poem becomes a form of conversation between the poet and 'You' who is, perhaps, his mother or, maybe, God. What is clear is that

Celan cannot write without being conscious of his own Jewishness and what happened to the Jewish people during the war, but this quest to speak of what is unspeakable becomes an example of what happens when the tragedy of the Holocaust strips away all possibility of sentimentality but you still have to say something or try to say something, even if this is only, in Celan's language, a breath or a crystal.

Here is his poem 'Tenebrae'.

> Near are we, Lord,
> near and graspable.
>
> Grasped already, Lord,
> clawed into each other, as if
> each of our bodies were
> your body, Lord.
>
> Pray, Lord,
> pray to us,
> we are near.
>
> Wind-skewed we went there,
> went there, to bend
> over pit and crater.
>
> Went to the water-trough, Lord.
>
> It was blood, it was
> what you shed, Lord.
> It shined.
>
> It cast your image into our eyes, Lord.
> Eyes and mouth stand so open and void, Lord.
> We have drunk, Lord.
> The blood and the image that was in the blood, Lord.
>
> Pray, Lord.
> We are near.[8]

Here we can see something of the conversation that Celan speaks about, this time explicitly with someone called 'Lord'. It is certainly an angry poem where we have to drink the wrath of God, and it deliberately reverses the language of Psalm 145.18, 'The Lord is close to those who call upon him.' Here God has to pray to us who are dying, whose bodies are clawed into each other as they were in the death camps. The title, 'Tenebrae' comes from the old liturgy of Holy Week where gradually, one after another candles are put out as Good Friday approaches, and so it aligns dead Jews with Christ crucified. Chagall did the same in his painting *The White Christ*, where the crucified Jesus wears a Jewish prayer shawl. What is important about the poem is the sense of reversal, where God now is vulnerable; but also the relationship between God and the speaker of the poem is one simply of movement, of attention and movement, not one of rational description or argument. Nothing of that kind can be envisaged after 20 January.

In another poem the conversation is still present but the 'other' is less clear, indeed has become no-one. The poem is called 'Psalm'.

> No one kneads us again out of earth and clay,
> no one incants our dust.
> No one.
>
> Blessèd art thou, No One.
> In thy sight would
> we bloom.
> In thy
> spite.
>
> A Nothing
> we were, are now, and ever
> shall be, blooming:
> the Nothing – , the
> No-One's-Rose.
>
> With
> our pistil soul-bright,
> our stamen heaven-waste,
> our corona red

from the purpleword we sang
over, O over
the thorn.[9]

In this poem Celan moves directly into the via negativa. Who God is cannot be spoken of, we know him only as No-One. Although God is No-One, there is such pressure, as it were, from No-One that he cannot be ignored. He has to be spoken of and, indeed, spoken to. At the same time various biblical points of contact are present – the creation, where God breathed life into dust and created Adam and also the crucifixion once again with the reference to thorn, the red corona or crown of the flower and the colour purple, which was the colour of Christ's robe. Here is emptiness and death but also, at the same time, lament and possible promise, but only because of and after the death. Once again the classical God, the known God has disappeared and becomes the unknown God of the negative way, unspoken of and unspeaking but inevitably present. This God is known and discovered via the route of suffering and death.

Paul Celan found himself caught between the necessity of saying something and the inability to say anything in the face of the horror of the Holocaust. Can he even speak of God in these circumstances? But if he does not speak does he not lapse into total nullity? As we have seen George Steiner has pointed out that Celan is a representative of a particular phenomenon. He is not alone in his dilemma.

> In Kafka's prose, in the poetry of Paul Celan or of Mandelstam, in the messianic linguistics of Benjamin and in the aesthetics and political sociology of Adorno, language operates, self-doubtingly, on the sharp edge of silence. . . . The consequences and correlatives of these great philosophical-psychological underminings and of the western experience of uttermost political inhumanity, are ubiquitous. . . . At decisive points, ours is today a civilisation 'after the word'.[10]

In his dilemma Celan reaches back into the mystical tradition of his faith and links his dilemma with that of the mystics themselves. We shall see that Etty Hillesum does a similar thing with the scriptural and theological traditions of Christianity in order to make some degree of sense of what is happening to her during the Nazi occupation of Amsterdam. What is surprising is that so few Christian theologians of any merit have followed the same path and have grappled with the impact of the Holocaust on the way in which they speak of God. During the war itself it was Dietrich Bonhoeffer who began to grapple with these issues in his *Letters and Papers from Prison* and, to some extent in his *Ethics*, but, tragically, he was prevented by the Nazis from continuing to develop his thinking. There are some signs now, so many years later, and under the urgent influence of postmodern thinkers, who themselves write in the knowledge of and in the face of the breakdown of modernism, that things are changing. Professor David Ford calls for a greater recognition of the need to do theology after Auschwitz in an essay *Apophasis and the Shoah*, where he begins to sketch out some ways in which Christians who wish to speak about Jesus Christ can also speak of the Holocaust. He says that Christians who face Jesus Christ must also be with Jesus Christ as he faces the horror of Auschwitz and who 'is silent, who listens to cries, who is self effacing, suffers violence and dies'. He continues,

> To face Jesus Christ means learning to be responsible before him, learning to be judged by him, to look on others as he looks on them, to have 'the mind of Christ', to be vigilant, and to speak and be silent in his Spirit. . . . If anything is clear from Jesus' own teaching about God's future it is that those who are most confident that they have worked it out are likely to be most surprised. This above all is the place for reserve, for an agnostic yet expectant silence which is open to the unexpected.[11]

This, in many ways, is precisely what Etty Hillesum found herself able to do, and she surprised herself and those who loved her, in the process.

The story of Etty Hillesum is becoming better known. She was born of educated Jewish parents in Middelburg in the Netherlands in 1914. She read law and Slavic languages at the University of Amsterdam in the late 1930s and moved in somewhat left-wing bohemian circles. She admits that she had many lovers and was practised at the art of love, but still senses an inner confusion or lack of direction in her life. In 1941 she met Julius Spier, a psychochirologist, who had been trained by Jung. He introduced her to the Bible, Hebrew and Christian Scriptures, as well as Augustine, and taught her to deal with her own depressive tendencies. She lived openly as a Jewish woman in Amsterdam at the same time that Anne Frank was hiding in her attic and, like Anne Frank, kept a diary. In 1942 she began work for the Jewish Council in the city. This was the body which was established by the occupying powers to deal with Jewish questions. The Jewish people of the Netherlands were being systematically deported to the death camps and many went through the transit camp at Westerbork. Etty asked to be transferred to work there. She became ill and came back to Amsterdam but insisted on returning. She received offers to go into hiding but believed, like Edith Stein, that she must 'share her people's fate' and consistently refused to disappear. By July 1943 she was permanently at Westerbork, and in the autumn she and her family were sent to Auschwitz, where she died on 30 November. A postcard was dropped from the train in which she travelled which read, 'We left the camp singing.'

Her diaries only cover the years 1941–2. Extracts from them, together with a number of her letters from Westerbork, have been published in English,[12] but more recently the Etty Hillesum Foundation has published a new English translation of the full text of her diaries and all of the known letters.[13] Her diary has become important spiritual reading for both Jews and Christians, especially those interested in developing a spirituality for women. It is also a firsthand record of suffering under the extremes of Nazi occupation and the threat of death. The diary is important psychologically because it shows how the human person can develop positively even in dire circumstances, but it is primarily an important theological text because it demonstrates how the soul can bear and relate to God at its deepest level and lose its 'self' in the awareness of and participation in this inner divine presence even in the face of the most extreme deprivation.

Etty's reaction to her circumstances is perhaps best understood by a series of extracts from her writings. The diaries begin with her inner distress:

> I am accomplished in bed, just about seasoned enough I should think to be counted among the better lovers, and love does indeed suit me to perfection, and yet it remains a mere trifle, set apart from what is truly essential, and deep inside me something is still locked away . . . deep down something like a tightly-wound ball of twine binds me relentlessly . . .[14]

But her relationship with Julius Spier, whom she calls 'S', and which had a very strong sexual element, deepens her, and she is glad to record her growing awareness of God:

> Last night, cycling through cold, dark Lairesse Straat – if only I could repeat everything I babbled out then! Something like this: 'God, take me by your hand, I shall follow you dutifully, and not resist too much. I shall evade none of the tempests life has in store for me, I shall try to face it as best as I can. . . . I shall try to spread some of my warmth, of my genuine love for others, wherever I go . . .[15]

This process continues and grows into an almost physical force or power which overwhelms her. She becomes 'the girl who learned to kneel', and she writes,

> Last night, shortly before going to bed, I suddenly went down on my knees in the middle of this large room, between the steel chairs and the matting. Almost automatically. Forced to the ground by something stronger than myself. Some time ago

I said to myself, 'I am a kneeler in training.' I was still embarrassed by this act, as intimate as gestures of love that cannot be put into words either, except by a poet . . . S. once said to me that it took quite a long time before he dared to say 'God', without feeling that there was something ridiculous about it. Even though he was a believer. . . . 'The girl who could not kneel.' This morning, in the grey dawn, in a fit of nervous agitation, I suddenly found myself on the floor, huddled up, my head on the ground. As if I were trying to seize peace by force.[16]

Later in some beautiful passages she records how she came to know the real meaning of sorrow:

Living and dying, sorrow and joy, the blisters on my feet and the jasmine behind the house, the persecution, the unspeakable horrors – it is all as one in me, and I accept it as one mighty whole. . . . Give your sorrow all the space and shelter in your-self that is its due, for if everyone bears his grief honestly and courageously, the sorrow that now fills this world will abate . . . And if you will have given sorrow the space its gentle origins demand, then you may truly say: life is beautiful and so rich. So beautiful and so rich that it makes you want to believe in God.[17]

Importantly, at the same time as she learned the real meaning of sorrow she also came to know something of the vulnerability of God. Like Paul Celan she speaks of God as needing us:

You cannot help us, but we must help You and defend Your dwelling place inside us to the last . . . no one is in their clutches who is in your arms . . . I shall never drive You from my presence . . . You can see, I look after You, I bring You not only my tears and my forebodings on this stormy, gray Sunday morning, I even bring You scented jasmine. And I shall bring You all the flowers I shall meet on my way, and truly there are many of these. I shall try to make You at home always. . . . I thank You for the great gift of being able to read people. Sometimes they seem to me like houses with open doors. I walk in and

113

roam through passages and rooms, and every house is furnished a little differently and yet they are all of them the same, and every one must be turned into a dwelling dedicated to You, oh God. And I promise You, yes, I promise that I shall try to find a dwelling and a refuge for You in as many houses as possible. There are so many empty houses, and I shall prepare them all for You, the most honoured lodger. Please forgive this poor metaphor.[18]

And the diary ends with the words,

I have broken my body like bread and shared it out among men. And why not, they were hungry and had gone without for so long. . . . We should be willing to act as a balm for all wounds.[19]

Some have questioned just how genuine all this is. It is said to contain an element of fabrication and many have said that it is simply not possible to come to such a conclusion in the face of the horror of the Holocaust. Does Etty's writing possess a genuine integrity? How can somebody who is faced daily by death and destruction, speak in this way? We asked the same question in our reflections on the work of Julian of Norwich. How can such an optimistic vision be possible in the face of death? Tzvetan Todorov, the eminent French philosopher, in his book *Facing the Extreme*, examined many of the recorded responses to the Holocaust and other similar terrible events and in his analysis of Etty's writing finds her seriously wanting. He says,

Even though I may not believe in the possibility of a world without evil or suffering, I do not agree that we should welcome every evil and every suffering as though they were fated to be, as though they were all part of cosmic harmony.[20]

Others have wondered whether Etty's work is a kind of spiritual fiction, a series of artificial cameos put together in order to create an acceptable account of what is happening to her in the darkness. They point out that it cannot be said that Etty really lived as a Jew and so although so much of her writing is full of scriptural resonances any attempt to assimilate her to the Jewish mystical or religious tradition must be treated with extreme care. It is clear she found as much inspiration in Rilke as in Augustine. Nor did she draw the same parallels between the crucifixion of Christ and the slaughter of the Jews as Paul Celan. Tina Beattie, in an insightful and intelligent assessment of Etty and the criticisms which have been made of her, writes,

> Hillesum presents something of a dilemma. Perhaps we have to understand her as a mystic who does not write within a tradition, but that tradition is itself the syncretistic one of post-Enlightenment European culture, which was being torn apart in the last years of Hillesum's life. . . . She offers a post-religious spirituality grounded in humanist scholarship and private prayer, but not supported by religious rituals, structures, institutions. Her understanding of God owes as much to psychotherapy and literature as to theology.[21]

But Tina Beattie goes on to say that she believes this vision to be genuine, that it is a genuine person who writes here and that she personally 'owns' the wisdom she writes of so fluently and that the God of whom she speaks is not simply a convenient or cosmetic literary fiction.

> It is truly a dialogue with another, with the Other, and in the end it is only this Other that allows her to believe that there is still meaning and truth in the world.[22]

Ultimately Etty found that the world was meaningless without faith in what she cannot but call God. Although the expression of that faith was very much determined by her reading it was nonetheless a genuine apprehension, and the text of her diary cannot really be read in any other way without mis-hearing that integrity. Her vision is profoundly optimistic and very redolent of both Julian and Eckhart. It is deeply contemplative and participatory. It abandons classically expressed theologies in favour of a theology of presence and our redemptive participation in that presence. While Tina Beattie rightly warns Christians to respect the Jewish limits of her faith, her acceptance of vulnerability and the awareness that she carried within her a small and vulnerable God can only bring to mind, whatever Etty's own intentions, the response of Mary the Mother of Christ to the visitation of the angel and to the acceptance by Christ of his vulnerability at the crucifixion. Is not what she said and did all of a piece and is this not Christlike? In one sense what Etty did was what Thomas, the character in Sebastian Faulks' novel whom we recalled in the first chapter of this book, asked us to do, that is to wake up to different possibilities. She was not given answers but a differ-ent way of seeing things, one which enabled her to care for those who were being driven insane by the threat of death but also to live her life as a form of 'extended rapture'. She found that to accept and live by a new way of being 'self', when 'self' is defined as 'movement towards the other' or 'welcome to the other'; and to accept and practise a new way of speaking where language is defined as 'word out of silence', was to live theolo-gically, that is 'before God'.[23] This is what Etty acted out and what Paul Celan wrote into his poems. Celan could not write the name of God with any ease or comfort and Etty admitted how difficult it was and had to be brought to her knees before she could do so, but nonetheless that is what they were brought to. It is a pity that so many theologians, both Jewish and Christian, have not been brought to the same point. One question we are left with is whether it is only an awareness of suffering which delivers us from old and inadequate ways of speaking about the transcendent or living our lives in a different way?

A Balm for All Wounds

We should be willing to act as a balm for all wounds.
                                   Etty Hillesum (October 1942)

The scent of jasmine was her favourite smell.
In Amsterdam it wafted on the breeze.

Paul Celan and Etty Hillesum

. . . and still life will be beautiful, she wrote,
always beautiful. Impassive trees
in line along the edge of the canal.
The gliding motion of a narrowboat.

From within the barbed wire of the place
they sent her to, she watched a soldier pick
wild flowers, herself a lily of the field
to reassure the frightened and the sick
by staying calm. She took her leave with grace
and wrote these words although the truck was sealed:

We left the camp singing.

Philip Lyons

6

Conclusion:
'. . . til you go out of yourself'

———•◆•———

In the second series of his *Centuries* Thomas Traherne wrote these words:

> We infinitely wrong ourselves by laziness and confinement. All creatures in all nations, and tongues, and people praise God infinitely; and the more, for being your sole and perfect treasures. You are never what you ought till you go out of yourself and walk among them.[1]

In this little set of sentences Traherne reaches back into the past and on into the future of the mystical way. Here he reaches right back into the New Testament and the words of Jesus, 'For those who want to save their life will lose it, and those who lose their life for my sake will find it.'[2] He also reaches back to the call for self-annihilation found in Eckhart, and the discovery of the indwelling Lord found in Julian. Above all he reaches forward: to the crisis of the self in the twentieth century, the demand of postmodern thinkers such as Emmanuel Levinas to recognize the unknown in others and in the self, and to the way in which the speaker of Paul Celan's poetry reaches out in a dialogue with whoever it is that 'you' represents. He also, unnervingly, foreshadows the words of Etty Hillesum as she walks among the almost dead in Westerbork and says,

> I thank you for the great gift of being able to read people. Sometimes they seem to me like houses with open doors. I walk

in and roam through passages and rooms, and every house is furnished a little differently and yet they are all of them the same, and every one must be turned into a dwelling dedicated to You, oh God. And I promise You, yes, I promise that I shall try to find a dwelling and a refuge for You in as many houses as possible. There are so many empty houses, and I shall prepare them all for You, the most honoured lodger.[3]

All of these writers have discovered that in order to be truly yourself you have to abandon your 'self' and walk out in thankfulness and praise. Thomas Merton, the American monk, speaks of how when reading Traherne we must 'penetrate immediately to the central intuition, a basic Eucharistic and primitive Christian theology of praise'.[4]

Merton's point is a real one – that the mystical way is a way of praise and thankfulness and so derives from and is integral to the believer's participation in a liturgical and Eucharistic community of praise. It is not an esoteric and private way but an opening of the inner eye to the glory of life as embedded in God. One thing the mystic writers do not do is entertain some sort of distinction between what we might call 'religious' awareness and the ordinary everyday experience of life. We might call the latter secular. The writers we have been concerned to examine do not do that. They find that the world is set in an extraordinarily intimate relationship with God. It is embedded in God and God in it. To know this is to bring us to the point of thankfulness and praise. Oliver Davies, in writing about the medieval European mystical tradition, warns us that unless we understand this we shall misread the mystical texts and think that they are about some sort of transcendental experience which is more a preoccupation of modern people than it was for the mystics of the past. He says,

And so, failing to grasp the extent to which – for Eckhart and other medieval mystics – the world was itself set in the most intimate relation to God, we take him to be talking about a form of transcendental knowledge or 'experience' which is quite other than ordinary knowing rather than being its most essential root and core.[5]

So these writers are not asking us to discover something different but to open our eyes to what already is within and around us, to catch sight of what Davies calls 'the most essential root and core' of our knowing, namely that we are set in God's world and that, as Julian says, nothing can be amiss. Then we shall see something 'different' because we shall see the way in which all things are already in God. This is the unfailing message of Traherne, who constantly repeats the refrain 'you will never enjoy the world aright . . .', continuing with a number of 'untils' and different admonitions to open our eyes to the way things really are but which in our blindness we cannot see.

We have, of course, been prevented from understanding the mystics in this way by a number of factors. One of them is the legacy of past misinterpretation, mainly based on the work of William James and then supported by writers such as Evelyn Underhill. For them mysticism was a separate category of experience which to their minds was a form of proof of God's existence. If people had these mystical experiences, and they believed the texts showed that they did, then these experiences were a guarantee of the existence of God when all else appeared to have failed in the face of the totalizing scientific explanations current at the time. But William James and Evelyn Underhill read the texts in the light of their own needs. They were rather like the early anthropologists (who were actually contemporaries of James) who were delighted to know that African tribes were different but who never went to see them. James and his followers neglected to read the texts in their social, political and theological contexts. This has now been corrected and the results show that there is a disjunction between the texts and our twentieth-century reading of them. We have read into them something of our own wishes and needs. Meanwhile the totalizing scientific explanations which caused James and others to run for the cover of mystical experience have also been called into question. Science is a far more open science than it was.

The flip-side of this misinterpretation is that we have rejected the texts precisely because the texts are seen as esoteric. We have agreed with James and others that they are 'mystical' and contain a record of mystical experience but we have not wanted a mystical religion. In the face of the same scientism which forced James into seeing the texts as evidence of an unassailable way into God, we have said that we do not want an unassailable God, rather we want a rational God that every rational man or woman can believe in. The result is that the texts have been ignored. They have been classified as obsolete and 'medieval' in the quest for a 'rational' faith. So we have also been prevented from understanding the mystical texts by our modernist mindset.

All this has meant that we have allowed the texts and their authors to be misinterpreted because of our need for certainty of one kind or another. We were blinded to their meaning either by our desire to see the texts as certain evidence of a special religious experience, the existence of which provided an experiential proof of the existence of God; or by our belief that only rational religion was acceptable in our day and these texts were certainly evidence of something irrational and medieval. Either way they remained unread and unavailable. This has meant that it is only now, now when we are faced with the breakdown of the modern and the rational, what George Steiner calls 'the retreat from the word', that we are, perhaps, able to re-enter the world of the mystical writers and understand them as they were written. The conditions now exist for a resurrection of these texts and a dissemination of their difference in a world which accepts difference and allows us to live by it. Not only has the postmodern now proved its worth to the Church by providing the climate in which the meaning of these texts can be unlocked, but the irony is that if only the Church had kept reading these texts and guarded their meaning and their value intact, then it would not, perhaps, have found the postmodern world so difficult to understand or so alien. There has been so much ink shed and opportunities missed because the Church has found the postmodern climate of opinion alien. But the fact that the postmodern period now allows us to read the texts so happily and clearly should be an object lesson to people of faith not to abandon the texts of the past in such a hurry next time around.

But in these postmodern days, once we can see that human identity is not guaranteed by possession of and adherence to the 'self' but indeed that adherence to that 'self' can ultimately destroy who we are, then we are set free to discover ourselves in relationship and in participation. Then we may rediscover that we are embedded in God and become the sort of people the mystics – if that is indeed the correct title for them – believed we should be. This is, of course, a risky enterprise, because we may not discover or rediscover any such thing, and postmodern writers are themselves divided between those who do rediscover God in this way and those who do not. Consequently ecclesial authority is proving very cautious about letting people loose in the postmodern world to lose or find God for themselves. It prefers to give them the old classical certainties in the old formularies and ask them simply to accept that these are true or to continue to try to find reasons why the old formularies are true. The trouble is that postmodernism is far too pervasive now and such a strategy will clearly be seen as embattled and defensive and will be quickly abandoned by those whom it is designed to protect.

Some of the struggle of the institutional Church to come to terms with this situation can be seen in some contemporary Christian writers, especially those who have sought to find some meaning in the classical expressions of the faith but have been defeated and are looking for alternatives. An interesting example of this is the book *Humane Christianity* by Alan Bartlett. This is an extensive and considered attempt to rediscover a way of talking about God in the face of what Bartlett calls 'Inhumane Christianity'. Inhumane Christianity is represented by those attempts to talk about God which espouse an unnecessary supernaturalism, exercise excessive and inappropriate authority, consider the essential flaw in humanity to be a pride of will which should be broken, and deny the goodness of creation. This creates a Church which is

> hostile to human desires and careless about human dignity, indifferent to a full life in this world but also too closely allied to existing unequal human power structures and authoritarian in its attitudes and practices.[6]

We might also say that it would be a Church which used a classical, descriptive style of theological talk and which assumed, by and large, that it knew the truth about Christian doctrine. In the face of such an inhumane style of faith Bartlett attempts to formulate what he calls

> a reappraisal of elements of the classic Christian spiritual disciplines in the light of current theological insights, a theological reading of church history and contemporary missiological needs.[7]

This is well intended, as the 'inhumane' Christianity of which Bartlett speaks is certainly the product of an over-assertive rationalism which now needs to be restated and re-evaluated in the light of the tradition it purports to represent. To some extent that has been the aim of this book. Bartlett also looks at the spiritual traditions and turns to Benedict, Bede and Francis in his search for a simpler faith, to Richard Hooker in his quest for a theology of human dignity, to Julian of Norwich, Martin Luther and Jeremy Taylor in search for a greater joy in bodiliness, the Desert Fathers for greater stability and patience and so on. He is right to try to return to the earlier premodern writers for a theology in which to restate the faith today.

And in that he is partially successful. The last pages of the book reveal what the author believes to be the principle characteristics of such a humane Christianity, namely: the essential goodness of God's creation and humanity as the pinnacle of that creation; this creation is essentially glorious; the core of God and his action is love; the atonement is essentially an absorbing of evil which liberates us to a life of love and so on. Such a faith discriminates in its use of Scripture and knows that it is not released from heartbreak, but seeks to model what is fully human on the life of Christ. There are many people who have embraced the faith through a classical evangelical conversion who then have to move through the difficulties that they find in that faith to lay hold on the authentic catholic Christian tradition which Bartlett describes and which celebrates the life-giving nature of God's continuous activity.

The difficulty with Bartlett's exposition is not its intention but its incompleteness. It simply does not reach far enough into the postmodern condition in which most people now find themselves. He espouses and expounds a faith in the goodness and love of God but leaves it at precisely that point, as an exposition, as a faith which we must think about, find rationally more acceptable and then adopt and believe in. The one point which he neglects in the spiritual tradition of which he speaks is the one point which is necessary, which is the matter of *participation*.[8] For the writers we have been considering the essential point is that the faithful person enters into the being of God, or finds they are already within the being of God, or God living within them. They find themselves as part of the Trinity and so part of a universe of praise and thanksgiving. No real attention is given by Bartlett to this dimension of the traditions he talks about, and consequently his faith remains more objective than it should do. He has not heeded Eckhart's words,

> When we turn away from ourselves and from all created things, to that extent we are united and sanctified in the soul's spark, which is untouched by either space or time. This spark

125

is opposed to all creatures and desires nothing but God, naked, just as he is in himself.[9]

Nor has he heeded the words of Julian of Norwich,

> I saw the soul as wide as it were an endless citadel, and also as it were a blessed kingdom . . . In the midst of that city sits our Lord Jesus, true God and true man . . . He sits erect there in the soul, in peace and in rest, and he rules and guards heaven and earth and everything that is.[10]

Nor does he seem to share Traherne's' perception,

> But now there is an infinite union between Him and us, He being infinitely delightful to us, and we to Him.[11]

Nor has he discovered Etty's promise of the divine lodger,

> And I promise You, yes, I promise that I shall try to find a dwelling and a refuge for You in as many houses as possible. There are so many empty houses, and I shall prepare them all for You, the most honoured lodger.[12]

All of these speak of a theology of participation in God, and in the end it is only such a theology which will not just convince men and women in the present age of the existence of God but also enable them to participate in that life. And it is precisely this postmodern age which enables us to perceive the truth of that as the older patterns of rational conviction and persuasion fade away. Implicit in the language and style of Bartlett's book there is something which says that you can argue people out of the inhumane faith which they have so long as you can state the case for a humane faith rationally enough. That does not go far enough, for the breakdown of the old ways is more extensive than Bartlett allows. Freud and Jung have done their work and old rationalisms cannot be recovered quite so easily as all that. He has to dig deeper into the past as well as deeper into the postmodern condition in which we find ourselves.

But it is not enough to state that. There is something else which needs to be said. In the end the mystical writers we have considered in this book are talking about a recovery of our sense of being embedded, along with the whole created order, in the life of God. They claim that we are somehow unable to see that this is the case and that the faithful liturgical life enables a kind of reawakening to our actual condition. They also claim, I would say, or at least certainly Eckhart claims, that much in religious practice is an obscuring of our condition, it colludes with our inner alienation and too much concentration upon it as a good in itself makes it even more difficult for us to be awakened to what is. Involved in this reawakening is a real self-forgetfulness, a loosening of the ties between us and our ego-selves so that identity is found by belonging in relationship rather than by asserting individual needs and rights. Belonging can also collude with the need of the ego-self and so even religion must come under careful scrutiny and its dangers be revealed. This self-forgetfulness and reawakening has echoes in other faith traditions, particularly Buddhism and to some extent Judaism, both of which emphasize the need to follow a path of simplicity of action, a *praxis* or rather an orthopraxis, rather than an orthodoxy, of belief. Perhaps if all faiths had followed a true orthodoxy, simply, what Thomas Merton calls 'a basic Eucharistic and primitive Christian theology of praise', rather than focusing on an orthodoxy of belief, some of our difficulties would have been avoided.

All of this is encapsulated in what happened at a Lenten discussion group which occurred in one of my parishes when I was a parish priest. There we were discussing the psalms, and in particular the psalms about the creation. One woman, an intelligent and traditionally minded person, suddenly began to tell the group about an experience she had had some years before. At that time the whole world seemed to her to be transformed. Everything seemed to shine with some sort of divine light, even the stones and the buildings and the people she met. All was alive with the light of God. She recounted this as if it were perfectly normal and talked about how after it her faith had been more settled. Now I was surprised. This was a reasonably conservative parish in the heart of the Church of England, somewhere where new liturgies and the physical giving of the peace presented difficulties. But I should not have been surprised, for the evidence of research into religious experience shows that this sort of thing happens all of the time and it happens to people outside as well as inside the Church.

Such moments of self-forgetfulness and reawakening, if that is what they are, are deeply positive, they result in a deeply positive understanding of the creation at large and, indeed, of the self in particular as part of the creation. Second, these moments are not self-generated. They come from somewhere else or someone else. Moreover, all of the accounts of these moments indicate that there is something which obscures or hides this deeper reality or person to whom we all belong. Something needs to fall away, and this is variously described as sin or illusion or something similar. There has to be a falling away of scales from the eyes.

What these moments are, I believe, are moments of total praise and total self-forgetfulness. They involve a total wakefulness, moments when we awake out of illusion and selfishness, out of self-concern and fear and see reality as it truly is and become who we truly are. This is what the mystical writers have been talking about all of the time. These are not private visions restricted to a religious elite, but glimpses of the truth of things accessible to all who accept the discipline of regular practice. Karen Armstrong was a Catholic nun who left the convent and lost her faith but then regained a deeper faith, this time a faith based upon a wakefulness to the reality of God in and through all things and all moments, a faith where compassion and what she calls a 'dethroning of the self' go hand in hand. She writes of it movingly in her autobiographical memoir, *The Spiral Staircase*:

> Religion is not about accepting twenty impossible propositions before breakfast but about doing things that change you. If you

behave in a certain way you will be transformed. Men and women have a potential for the divine and are not complete unless they realize it within themselves. Someone once asked the Buddha whether he was a god, a spirit or an angel. I am none of these, the Buddha replied, I am awake![13]

Several things follow. One is a total moral settledness. At this point the soul has not only returned home but has also rein-habited its moral dimension. Goodness flows. Life becomes a gift, every moment contains transcendence. It becomes almost impossible to harm or spoil things. Justice becomes a burning desire. Indeed, the saints also say that unless justice and mercy become a burning desire then nothing real has happened, no vision, no wakefulness, has occurred. Wakefulness without moral transformation is sleepwalking. And this is reflected in the accounts of the transfiguration in the Gospels. At this point Jesus becomes morally settled and can turn to and accept the suffering that he is to endure and urges his disciples to do the same. Acceptance of the cross becomes possible – and this is the one point on which all the accounts of the transfiguration agree, however different they are in other respects. Now Jesus can turn and bear the suffering of the world, to struggle for justice to the end, and asks us to do the same.

Earlier in this book we talked about Annie Dillard, the young American biologist who spent a whole year alone in the Shenandoah Valley looking at and studying the creation. She talks about two ways of seeing, one which is simply recording, as if the eye were a camera, and the other which involves an inner letting go. This way of seeing is, she says, the result of long spiritual discipline. When it happens, she says, it is less like seeing

> than like being for the first time seen, knocked breathless by a powerful glance . . . When I see this way I see truly.[14]

Effectively, you are woken up and God is.

Notes

1 The promise of postmodernity

1 Emmanuel Levinas, *Collected Philosophical Papers*, cited by Gerald L. Bruns, 'The Concepts of Art and Poetry in Emmanuel Levinas's Writings', in *The Cambridge Companion to Levinas*, ed. S. Critchley and R. Bernasconi (Cambridge: Cambridge University Press, 2002).
2 Exodus 3.14.
3 Exodus 33.18ff.
4 Genesis 3.10.
5 Exodus 20.18–19.
6 John Fenton, *More About Mark* (London: SPCK, 2001).
7 Mark 16.8.
8 Fenton, *More About Mark*, p. 55.
9 Sebastian Faulks, *Human Traces* (London: Hutchinson, 2005), p. 512.
10 Denys Turner, *Faith Seeking* (London: SCM Press, 2002), p. 42.
11 Turner, *Faith Seeking*, p. 46.

2 Meister Eckhart and the negative way

1 Matthew Paris, *Chronica Majora*, cited by Bernard McGinn, in *Meister Eckhart and the Beguine Mystics*, ed. Bernard McGinn (New York: Continuum, 1997), p. 2.
2 Marguerite Porete, *The Mirror of Simple Souls*, 144.
3 Michael Sells, 'The Pseudo-Woman and the Meister', in McGinn, *Meister Eckhart and the Beguine Mystics*, p. 141.
4 McGinn, *Meister Eckhart and the Beguine Mystics*, p. 11.
5 Eckhart, *German Sermons*, no. 48, *Ein Meister Sprichet*.
6 Eckhart, *The Book of Divine Consolation*.
7 Oliver Davies, *Meister Eckhart, Mystical Theologian* (London: SPCK, 1991), p. 116.
8 Eckhart, *German Sermons*, no. 42.
9 Eckhart, *German Sermons*, no. 48.

10 Eckhart, *German Sermons*, no. 28.
11 Eckhart, *German Sermons*, no. 5b.
12 Eckhart, *On Detachment*.
13 Don Cupitt, *Mysticism after Modernity* (Oxford: Blackwell, 1998), p. 6.
14 Denys Turner, 'Material Poverty or Poverty of Spirit? Holiness and the Liberation of the Poor', in *Holiness Past and Present*, ed. Stephen C. Barton (London: T. & T. Clark, 2003), p. 458.
15 Rowan Williams, *On Christian Theology* (Oxford: Blackwell, 2000), ch. 1.
16 *The Cloud of Unknowing*, chapter 4.

3 Julian of Norwich and the body politic

1 Froissart, *Chroniques*, cited by R. B. Dobson, in *The Peasants' Revolt of 1381* (London: Macmillan, 1983).
2 *The Book of Margery Kempe* (there are various editions).
3 Frederick Christian Bauerschmidt, *Julian of Norwich and the Mystical Body Politic of Christ* (Notre Dame, Ind.: University of Notre Dame Press, 1999), p. 2.
4 Julian of Norwich, *Showings*, chapter 2. Chapter notation and quotations from Julian will be from the Long Text as translated by Colledge and Walsh in the series Classics of Western Spirituality (New York: Paulist Press, 1978).
5 *Showings*, chapter 2.
6 Mechthild of Magdeburg, *The Flowing Light of the Godhead*, 2.14, cited by Grace Jantzen in *Julian of Norwich: Mystic and Theologian*, 2nd edn (London: SPCK, 2000).
7 *Showings*, chapter 48.
8 Jantzen, *Julian of Norwich*, p. 61.
9 *Showings*, chapter 4.
10 *Showings*, chapter 4.
11 Hebrews 10.11.
12 *Showings*, chapter 1.
13 Jean-Luc Marion, *L'Idole et la distance: cinq études* (Grasset, 1977) p. 37, cited by Bauerschmidt, *Julian of Norwich*.
14 *Showings*, chapter 5.
15 Text of the edition by Marion Glasscoe (Exeter: University of Exeter, 1976).
16 *Showings*, chapter 5.

17 *Showings*, chapter 1.
18 *Showings*, chapter 11.
19 *Showings*, chapter 11.
20 *Showings*, chapter 27.
21 *Showings*, chapter 27.
22 *Showings*, chapter 27.
23 *Showings*, chapter 27.
24 *Showings*, chapter 40.
25 *Showings*, chapter 37.
26 William of St Thierry, *The Golden Epistle*, sections 257–8.
27 1 John 3.2.
28 John 7.38.
29 *Showings*, chapter 41.
30 *Showings*, chapter 43.
31 *Showings*, chapter 46.
32 *Showings*, chapter 46.
33 *Showings*, chapter 50.
34 *Showings*, chapter 51.
35 Bauerschmidt, *Julian of Norwich*, p. 178.
36 *Showings*, chapter 68.
37 See especially the work of Catherine Pickstock, *After Writing* (Oxford: Blackwell, 1998), and the work of the Radical Orthodoxy group.
38 Bauerschmidt, *Julian of Norwich*, p. 199.

4   Thomas Traherne and the reinvention of the world

1 Douglas Chambers, *The Reinvention of the World: English Writing 1650–1750* (London: Arnold, 1996).
2 Thomas Traherne, *A Sober View of Dr Twisses his Considerations*, section 27, in *The Works of Thomas Traherne*, vol. 1, ed. Jan Ross (Cambridge: D. S. Brewer, 2005), p. 186.
3 See A. M. Allchin, 'The Sacrifice of Praise and Thanksgiving', in *Profitable Wonders: Aspects of Thomas Traherne*, by A. M. Allchin, Anne Ridler and Julian Smith (Oxford: Amate Press, 1989).
4 Allchin, 'Sacrifice of Praise and Thanksgiving', p. 32.
5 Ross, *The Works of Thomas Traherne*, p. xiii.
6 Denise Inge, in *Thomas Traherne: Poetry and Prose, Selected and Introduced by Denise Inge* (London: SPCK, 2002), p. xx.

7 For these details and others see Denise Inge, *Thomas Traherne: Poetry and Prose*, and the essay by Anne Ridler in *Profitable Wonders*.
8 Thomas Traherne, *Centuries of Meditations*, 3.7. For the *Centuries* I quote from the 2nd edition of the text edited by Bertram Dobell, published by his son Philip in 1927.
9 *Centuries*, 3.41.
10 *Centuries*, 3.46.
11 *Centuries*, 1.29.
12 *Centuries*, 3.3.
13 Chambers, *Reinvention of the World*, ch. 6.
14 Henry Vaughan, 'The Retreat'.
15 Thomas Traherne, 'The Return'.
16 David F. Ford, *Self and Salvation: Being Transformed* (Cambridge: Cambridge University Press, 1999), p. 276.
17 Thomas Traherne, *Select Meditations*, ed. Julia Smith (Manchester: Carcanet Press, 1997), p. 75.
18 *Centuries*, 4.49.
19 *Centuries*, 1.42.
20 *Centuries*, 1.44.
21 Pseudo-Denys, *The Divine Names*, 712.
22 Denys Turner, *Eros and Allegory: Medieval Exegesis of the Song of Songs* (Kalamazoo, Mich.: Cistercian Publications, 1995), p. 41.
23 *Centuries*, 1.58.
24 *Centuries*, 1.60.
25 Thomas Traherne, 'The Kingdom of God', in Ross, *The Works of Thomas Traherne*, vol. 1.
26 'The Kingdom of God'.
27 John Polkinghorne, *Science and the Trinity* (London: SPCK, 2004).
28 Allchin, 'Sacrifice of Praise and Thanksgiving', p. 35.
29 Augustine, *The Literal Meaning of Genesis*, 12.3.15.
30 Mark A. McIntosh, *Discernment and Truth* (New York: Herder & Herder, 2004), p. 247. The whole of McIntosh's long exposition of Traherne is important reading.
31 McIntosh, *Discernment and Truth*, p. 248.
32 Denys Turner, *The Darkness of God: Negativity in Christian Mysticism* (Cambridge: Cambridge University Press, 1995), p. 20.
33 Edwin Muir, 'The Transfiguration', from *Collected Poems 1921–58* (London: Faber & Faber, 1960).

34 Annie Dillard, *Pilgrim at Tinker Creek* (New York: Harper & Row, 1974), p. 32.

35 Dillard, *Pilgrim at Tinker Creek*, p. 32.

36 Dillard, *Pilgrim at Tinker Creek*, p. 270.

37 A. Leigh DeNeef, *Traherne in Dialogue: Heidegger, Lacan, and Derrida* (Durham, NC: Duke University Press, 1988), p. 89.

5 'A balm for all wounds': Paul Celan and Etty Hillesum

1 George Steiner, *Language & Silence* (London: Faber & Faber, 1967), p. 40.

2 Martin Luther, *On the Jews and their Lies*, 47.267.

3 Thomas Merton, 'A Devout Meditation in Memory of Adolf Eichmann', in *Raids on the Unspeakable* (London: Burns & Oates, 1977), p. 30.

4 See especially the thought of Emmanuel Levinas and Chapter 1 of this book.

5 The essay by Rowan Williams, 'Theological Integrity', in *On Christian Theology* (Oxford: Blackwell, 2000), is particularly helpful and nuanced on this subject.

6 Paul Celan, 'Speech on the Occasion of the Award of the Georg Büchner Prize', in *Selected Poems and Prose of Paul Celan*, translated by John Felstiner (New York: W. W. Norton, 2001), p. 408.

7 Celan, 'Speech', p. 409.

8 Celan, *Selected Poems and Prose*, p. 103.

9 Celan, *Selected Poems and Prose*, p. 157.

10 George Steiner, in the essay 'Real Presences', reprinted in *No Passion Spent* (London: Faber & Faber, 1996), p. 24.

11 David Ford, 'Apophasis and the Shoah', in *Silence and the Word: Negative Theology and Incarnation*, ed. Oliver Davies and Denys Turner (Cambridge: Cambridge University Press, 2002), p. 198.

12 *An Interrupted Life: The Diaries of Etty Hillesum 1941–43* (London: Persephone Books, 1989).

13 *Etty: The Letters and Diaries of Etty Hillesum 1941–43*, complete and unabridged, ed. Klaas A. D. Smelik (Grand Rapids: Eerdmans, 2002).

14 *An Interrupted Life*, p. 1 (quotations are from the Washington Square Press edition, New York, 1985).

15 *An Interrupted Life*, p. 64.
16 *An Interrupted Life*, p. 76.
17 *An Interrupted Life*, p. 100.
18 *An Interrupted Life*, p. 215.
19 *An Interrupted Life*, pp. 242–3.
20 Tzvetan Todorov, *Facing the Extreme: Moral Life in the Concentration Camps*, English edition (London: Weidenfeld & Nicolson, 1999), p. 208.
21 Tina Beattie, 'Etty Hillesum: A Thinking Heart in a Darkened World', in *Spirituality and Society in the New Millennium*, ed. Ursula King with Tina Beattie (Brighton: Sussex Academic Press, 2001), p. 254.
22 Tina Beattie, 'Etty Hillesum', p. 255.
23 An important essay on the whole question of women's reaction to the Holocaust is to be found in 'Holiness In Extremis: Jewish Women's Resistance to the Profane in Auschwitz', by Melissa Raphael, in *Holiness Past and Present*, ed. Stephen Barton (London: T. and T. Clark, 2003).

6 Conclusion: '. . . til you go out of yourself'

1 Thomas Traherne, *Centuries of Meditations*, 2.76.
2 Matthew 16.25.
3 *An Interrupted Life: The Diaries of Etty Hillesum 1941–43* (New York: Washington Square Press, 1985), p. 215.
4 Thomas Merton, *Mystics and Zen Masters*, cited by A. M. Allchin in *Profitable Wonders* (Oxford: Amate Press, 1989), p. 35.
5 Oliver Davies, *God Within: The Mystical Tradition of Northern Europe*, rev. edn (London: Darton, Longman & Todd, 2006), p. xiv.
6 Alan Bartlett, *Humane Christianity* (London: Darton, Longman & Todd, 2004), p. 10.
7 Bartlett, *Humane Christianity*, p. xiii.
8 'Participation' is of particular importance to postmodern theologians and is well expounded by a number of them. See especially the essay 'Suspending the Material: The Return of Radical Orthodoxy' by John Milbank, Graham Ward and Catherine Pickstock in the important collection they edit, *Radical Orthodoxy: A New Theology* (Routledge, 1999). See p. 3, where they say, 'The central theological framework of radical

136

orthodoxy is "participation" as developed by Plato and reworked by Christianity, because any alternative configuration perforce reserves a territory independent of God.'

9 Eckhart, *German Sermons*, no. 48, *Ein Meister Sprichet.*
10 Julian of Norwich, *Showings*, chapter 68.
11 Traherne, *Centuries*, 4.49.
12 *An Interrupted Life*, p. 215.
13 Karen Armstrong, *The Spiral Staircase: A Memoir* (London: HarperCollins, 2004), p. 304. The whole of this memoir is worth reading.
14 Annie Dillard, *Pilgrim at Tinker Creek* (New York: Harper & Row, 1974), p. 32.

Both Alike to Thee
The Retrieval of the Mystical Way

MELVYN MATTHEWS

'The darkness and the light are both alike to thee' Psalm 139.12

The mystical way has largely been lost as an option within the mainstream life of the Church. We have turned the focus of our attention away from the immense reality of God. We have settled, perhaps, for something rather more comfortable.

In this ground-breaking and passionate book, Melvyn Matthews argues that believers today desperately need to retrieve a spiritual life of great depth in order to remain faithful in a world that contains much moral and social disintegration.

Both Alike to Thee affirms God, not just as an object of belief, but as the source of all being. It gives us a vision of the Church as the place where we can step out into his 'deep and dazzling darkness' with love and confidence.

'This is a very rich book, full of insight, of clear and challenging writing . . . [a] book whose resounding message must not go unheeded, for it takes us beyond words.'   ***Theology***

'A prophetic voice from within the institution! Melvyn Matthews is Chancellor of Wells Cathedral yet he points out that the mystical way has been lost as an option within the mainstream life of the Church. A remarkable book, written with great passion and deep feeling.'
Fellowship of Solitaries

Price : £9.99   ISBN-13: 978–0–281–05030–7
                                 ISBN-10: 0–281–05030–9

The Society for Promoting Christian Knowledge (SPCK) was founded in 1698. Its mission statement is:

To promote Christian knowledge by

- **Communicating the Christian faith in its rich diversity;**
- **Helping people to understand the Christian faith and to develop their personal faith; and**
- **Equipping Christians for mission and ministry.**

SPCK Worldwide serves the Church through Christian literature and communication projects in over 100 countries, and provides books for those training for ministry in many parts of the developing world. This worldwide service depends upon the generosity of others and all gifts are spent wholly on ministry programmes, without deductions.

SPCK Bookshops support the life of the Christian community by making available a full range of Christian literature and other resources, providing support for those training for ministry, and assisting bookstalls and book agents throughout the UK.

SPCK Publishing produces Christian books and resources, covering a wide range of inspirational, pastoral, practical and academic subjects. Authors are drawn from many different Christian traditions, and publications aim to meet the needs of a wide variety of readers in the UK and throughout the world.

The Society does not necessarily endorse the individual views contained in its publications, but hopes they stimulate readers to think about and further develop their Christian faith.

For further information about the Society, visit our website at *www.spck.org.uk* or write to:
SPCK, 36 Causton Street,
London SW1P 4ST, United Kingdom.